Contents

Environmental Regulation *and* Your Business

Environmental Regulation *and* Your Business

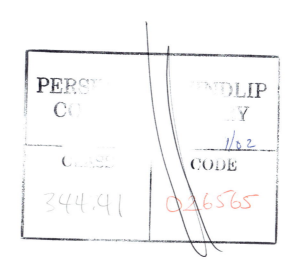
London: The Stationery Office

© The Stationery Office 2001

A CIP catalogue record for this book is available from the British Library.

A Library of Congress CIP catalogue record has been applied for
First published 2001

ISBN 0 11 702700 6

Printed on material containing 75% consumer waste and 25% ECF pulp.

Published by The Stationery Office Limited
and available from:

The Publications Centre
(Mail, telephone and fax orders only)
PO Box 276, London SW8 5DT
General enquiries 020 7873 0011
Telephone orders 020 7873 9090
Fax orders 020 7873 8200

The Stationery Office Bookshops
123 Kingsway, London WC2B 6PQ
020 7242 6393 Fax 020 7242 6394
68-69 Bull Street, Birmingham B4 6AD
0121 236 9696 Fax 0121 236 9699
33 Wine Street, Bristol BS1 2BQ
0117 9264306 Fax 0117 9294515
9-21 Princess Street, Manchester M60 8AS
0161 834 7201 Fax 0161 833 0634
16 Arthur Street, Belfast BT1 4GD
028 9023 8451 Fax 028 9023 5401
The Stationery Office Oriel Bookshop
18-19 High Street, Cardiff CF1 2BZ
029 2039 5548 Fax 029 2038 4347
71 Lothian Road, Edinburgh EH3 9AZ
0870 606 5566 Fax 0870 606 5588

Accredited Agents
(See Yellow Pages)

and through good booksellers

Printed in the UK by The Stationery Office Limited
TJ0005463 C00 11/01 655163 19585

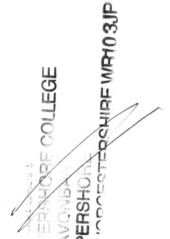

To Mary and Oscar

About the author

Declan Lyons, a scientist by qualification, worked in science, technology and industrial policy development before switching to journalism. He now specialises in business communications.

Declan runs his own communications consultancy, BCT Communications Ltd and provides consultancy and training services to a range of private and public sector organisations. He holds a BSc degree from University College, Dublin and an MBA from Trinity College, Dublin.

How to use this book

This book is broken into short, relatively self-contained chapters. You can choose to either read it straight through, or you can go immediately to the section that specifically interests you.

- If you want an overview of the environmental challenge, and of the necessary global response to it, **go to Chapter 2.**

- To find out about the European Union's role, **go to Chapter 3.**

  Chapter 4 introduces you to the British legislative process, whilst **Chapter 5** explains who does what within that process.

  Chapters 6 and 7 cover the main legislation in greater depth.

  In Chapters 8, 9 and 10, you will discover how to move from basic compliance to being able to boast green credentials.

  In the Appendix, you will find contact details for the top ten organisations to approach for further information and help.

Acknowledgements

I wish to acknowledge the help and co-operation given by a wide range of organisations and individuals. I thank the bodies listed below in particular for giving permission to reproduce parts of their publications or for preparing and supplying specific information.

BSI

The Environment Agency

Eco-label

Enfo

Envirowise

Greenleaf Publishing Ltd

Groundworks

Institute of Environmental Management and Assessment

People Seating Limited

Precious Metal Industries

I also acknowledge the help received from staff in Government Departments, particularly DEFRA and DTI, the European Union, particularly DG Environment and Netregs in the Environment Agency.

Introduction: The environmental challenge for the SME

'All the evidence of the last few years shows that there is going to be a lot of money in being green.' Dr James Watkins, Chief Executive of Kwikpower International[i]

The environment is important to business and is big business in its own right. It is vital that small- and medium-sized enterprises (SMEs) share the benefits of green business and avoid the pitfalls of environmental regulation. This book will help you to do just that.

WHAT THIS BOOK GIVES YOU

It would be hard to cover every aspect of each environmental regulation in one book – and even if it were possible, it is unlikely that those managing SMEs would have the time or the inclination to wade through such a text. This book provides an overview of the key issues and refers you to additional, supplementary sources where you will find any detailed information you may require that is specific to your business sector or area of interest.

We have written this book for business people who do not have access to their own in-house environmental specialists or specialist environmental expertise. Obviously, if you are involved in oil exploration or producing a range of toxic chemicals, you should have full-time specialists dealing with the environmental aspects of your business. Only a small number of companies have or need such expertise on tap. The vast majority must manage their environmental impacts as part of their business without the benefit of dedicated specialist staff; this book aims to make their life a bit easier.

WHAT WE DON'T COVER

This book focuses on the main legislation dealing with environmental issues relevant to SMEs. It does not cover specialist topics such as radioactive materials, control of major accident regulations or bioengineering. It also avoids planning and planning-related issues. The book touches on Northern Ireland and Scottish legislation but focuses on the English and Welsh regulatory framework.

GOOD BUSINESS NEEDS GOOD ENVIRONMENTAL MANAGEMENT

Effective managers know that they must take account of environmental issues when planning and operating their businesses. Excellent managers recognise that the growth in environmental awareness and regulation creates business opportunities for those companies ready to seize them. This book demonstrates how you can start reaping the business benefits of being green.

WHO IS IT FOR?

This book is written for those working in, or running, small- or medium-sized enterprises (SMEs). The Welsh European Funding Office captures the SME in a few simple bullet points. In their view, a company is an SME if:

- it has no more than 250 employees
- it has either an annual turnover not exceeding ECU 20 million, or a total balance sheet not exceeding ECU 10 million, and
- it is not more than 25 per cent-owned by one or more companies not fulfilling the criteria set out in the above definition, except public investment corporations, venture capital companies or, provided no control is exercised, institutional investors.

As a block, SMEs account for the vast majority of enterprises in the UK. In 1999, of an entire business population of 3.7 million enterprises, only 24,000 were medium-sized (50–249 employees), and less than 7,000 were large (250 or more employees). Small businesses, including those without employees, accounted for 98 per cent of all businesses, 45 per cent of non-government employment and (excluding the finance sector) 38 per cent of turnover.

SMEs account for a large proportion of UK business.[ii] It is hard to imagine that such a significant sector will be overlooked as environmental policies are turned into national and local regulations.

NOTES TO INTRODUCTION

i   Leo Lewis. 'Stores set to sell rubbish new petrol', *Independent on Sunday*, 24 June 2001, Kwikpower International makes clean-burning petrol from municipal waste.

ii Department of Trade and Industry Bulletin, 'Small and Medium Enterprises (SME) Statistics for the UK, 1999'.

CHAPTER 1

The world is what you make it

This chapter explains why two issues in particular, global warming and the depletion of the ozone layer, are important. It describes the problems we face and the proposals aimed at tackling them. It also mentions some of the other important international treaties affecting trade. Obviously, the European Union plays an important role in international environmental regulation. Given its particular importance for UK companies, we have devoted a separate chapter to it (see Chapter Two, following).

It is impossible to consider the environmental regulations that affect small- and medium-sized enterprises (SMEs) nationally without looking at what is happening to our planet as a whole. We begin by taking a world-view and try to identify the factors that will drive policy now and in the future. In particular, we will examine:

- climate change
- global warming
- greenhouse gases
- the Kyoto Protocol
- international treaties and their impact, and
- the broad approaches and principles underlying environmental regulation.

Each of these topics has the potential to change our businesses and our markets. Combined, they will be a major driving force for business globally and nationally.

Our challenge for the twenty-first century is to reduce the impact of human activity globally to ensure our continued survival and prosperity. At an international level, governments are uniting to develop a way of achieving this. The UK government has given emerging multilateral environmental agreements strong support. These international treaties now form either the framework or backdrop for much of our current environmental regulation. For companies engaged in international trade, these regulations are an integral part of their regulatory environment.

THE DRIVING FORCES FOR CHANGE

One swallow doesn't make a summer. However, when swallows begin to return to the British Isles earlier and earlier each year, as they are doing, we have to sit up and take notice. Our climate is changing. Some of these changes are almost imperceptible. We may welcome warmer summers, but other changes such as floods or droughts bring disastrous consequences for both individuals and for society.

Sometimes you don't need to be a fortune-teller to predict the future. It can be so obvious that we have little option but to face up to it. Climate change is now an eventuality and unless we change the way we think and act, we may destroy the very means by which we live.

WHY GREENHOUSE GASES ARE IMPORTANT

Increases in global greenhouse gas levels drive most of our climate change. These gases are the by-products of a wide range of industrial, commercial and consumer activities. Our global temperature depends upon a delicate balance of forces that keep it within a range that allows life to continue. Solar radiation strikes the Earth and is either absorbed or reflected back towards space. The Earth itself also radiates energy. Gases in the atmosphere absorb some of this radiated energy, giving rise to the greenhouse effect. As long as there is a balance between the energy coming in and that leaving, the temperature remains the same.

The Earth's energy balance began to change with increasing industrialisation. The greenhouse gases are carbon dioxide, methane, nitrous oxide, ozone and water vapour. Human activities are increasingly adding to the levels of these gases in the atmosphere – and at a rapid rate. For example, the levels of carbon dioxide have increased by approximately 25 per cent since pre-industrial times. Methane has increased even more rapidly. The increase in these gases results in more energy trapped on the Earth, causing a rise in global temperature. The Earth's temperature has increased by approximately 0.5°C (nearly 1°F) in the last century – most likely as a consequence of increasing greenhouse gas levels. More worrying is the fact that the temperature is increasing at an ever-faster rate and is likely to continue doing so in the future.

OZONE – AN IMPORTANT ISSUE

The changing levels in greenhouse gases are provoking global climatic effects. In addition, other emissions are damaging the ozone layer allowing greater ultraviolet light penetration. The ozone layer provides a protective shield against this damaging ultraviolet radiation. At ground level, ozone can be a toxic pollutant and is a key constituent of photochemical smog, but in the stratosphere, between eight and 50 kilometres (five to 31 miles) above us, it has a much more benign effect.

Ozone is a molecule composed of three atoms of oxygen. Stratospheric ozone plays a beneficial role by absorbing most of the biologically damaging ultraviolet sunlight (UV-B). The absorption of this radiation creates a heat source that actually forms the stratosphere. Over the past quarter of a century, scientists have observed that the ozone layer is thinning and, particularly above the poles, disappearing for periods. As a consequence, areas on the Earth, including the Northern Hemisphere, are experiencing increased levels of ultraviolet radiation.

Ultraviolet radiation is potentially lethal and, even at slightly increased levels, will cause damage to certain crops. UV radiation causes increased incidences of certain illnesses in humans and animals such as skin cancer, eye damage and depression of the immune system. The Government's Expert Group on Climate estimates that cases of skin cancer may increase in the UK by up to 30,000 a year – in part due to the impact of increased UV radiation.

A number of chemicals have been identified as causing damage to the ozone layer. These compounds contain various combinations of the chemical elements chlorine, fluorine, bromine, carbon and hydrogen and are often referred to as halocarbons. Some of the ozone-depleting gases have been used in applications such as refrigeration, air conditioning, foam blowing, cleaning of electronic components and as solvents. Another group are used in fire extinguishers.

'While enormous progress has been made over the past decade in phasing out ozone-destroying chemicals, the health of the ozone layer remains critical' according to Klaus Toepfer, Executive Director of the United Nations Environment Programme (UNEP) speaking at a meeting of world governments studying the impact of ozone depletion.[i]

The conference heard that satellite measurements taken in September 2000 revealed that the stratospheric ozone hole over the Antarctic had reached a record 28.3 million km^2 (11.1 million square miles). This is one million km^2 (391,000 square miles) more than the previous record in 1998. Earlier in 2000, ozone depletion over northern latitudes also reached record levels leading to predictions of a second ozone hole over the Arctic. Such an event would expose many millions of people to dangerous doses of ultraviolet-B radiation.

The UNEP believes that there is a danger that ozone-destroying chemicals are long lasting and take time to travel up to the stratosphere. Chemicals released years ago are still present in the atmosphere and are contributing to today's peak concentrations.

Meanwhile, global climate change is thought to be slowing the ozone layer's healing process. The warming of the atmosphere near the ground causes the stratosphere to become even colder. Cold stratospheric temperatures, particularly during the early Antarctic spring, catalyse the chemical processes that destroy ozone molecules.

CLIMATE CHANGE IS COUPLED WITH OTHER ENVIRONMENTAL PRESSURES

Climate change and ozone depletion are not taking place in a vacuum. They are occurring in a world where increasing level of pollutants are discharged into the seas and rivers, reducing our stock of clean water. Dumping of waste, soil contamination and over-farming are putting pressure on our land resource. Some of these activities, such as the destruction of tropical rain forests, speed up global warming by removing a valuable store of carbon and often releasing smoke, from tree-burning, into the atmosphere. In summary, we face a cocktail of environmental problems that can only be solved if we act quickly and decisively.

THE EXTENT OF OUR PROBLEMS

Scientific opinion may disagree about the detail, but in general the picture is clear. We can expect dramatic climatic change over the next thirty years. These changes will not simply be an inconvenience: they will radically alter the way that we live and work. A special United Nations Working Group[ii] projects that:

- crop yields will reduce
- flooding and droughts will become increasingly common
- the incidence of certain diseases such as malaria and cholera will rise markedly.

The Working Group observes that:

'The vulnerability of human societies and natural systems to climate extremes is demonstrated by the damage, hardship, and death caused by events such as droughts, floods, heat waves, avalanches, and windstorms. While there are uncertainties attached to estimates of such changes, some extreme events are projected to increase in frequency and/or severity during the twenty-first century due to changes in the mean and/or variability of climate, so it can be expected that the severity of their impacts will also increase in concert with global warming.'

In the UK, we face the threat of more frequent flooding with some low-lying areas disappearing altogether; wetter winters in some years will co-exist with water shortages in others. Increased ultraviolet light penetration will result in a greater number of skin cancers.

According to 'Climate Change: Draft UK Programme'[iii], globally seven out of the ten warmest years on record have been in the 1990s, with 1998 being the warmest to date. The climate could warm by approximately 3°C (5°F) over the next century. The resulting environmental problems will be of such a magnitude that they will absorb an increasing proportion of our resources, and this will result in a decline in life-quality for most of us.

Globally, some of our trading partners will face more serious problems. Severe climate change will have a greater impact in under-developed and developing economies. These pressures, coupled with global population growth, will place national economies under strain, interrupting supplies of basic raw materials thus impeding or paralysing international trade.

Addressing the Confederation of British Industry/Green Alliance Conference on the Environment held in October 2000, the Prime Minister, the Right Honourable Tony Blair, MP, outlined the threat that we now face:

- There are alarming changes in our atmosphere, in global temperatures, in weather patterns, in sea levels and in the protective ozone layer. As a result, across the world millions face drought, flooding, disease. Here in the UK, we, too, face threats – the prospect of exotic diseases becoming commonplace, of increased levels of skin cancer, of floods in some years, droughts in others, of low-lying areas being swallowed by the sea.
- Global population growth will put increased pressure on natural resources. The world population is set to rise from six billion to nine billion by 2050. So that economies across the world have the opportunity to develop, we must all use resources far more efficiently and switch to clean technologies.
- Fresh water is being polluted or simply used up. Demand is doubling every 21 years while supply is broadly unchanged.

- Soil degradation has affected two-thirds of the world's agricultural lands over the last 50 years, and the situation is getting worse.
- Half the world's wetlands have been lost over the past century and with them their unique plants and animals; and this is accelerating.
- One in ten of the world's tree species are at risk of extinction, and increasingly whole forest systems are under threat.
- Fishing fleets are still 40 per cent larger than the oceans can sustain and yet it (the fishing industry) still benefits from subsidies, worldwide.
- Here in the UK, farmland birds are disappearing; the house sparrow, once more cockney than the Cockneys, is now a rarity in London, and congestion means that urban traffic moves at the same speed as in 1890.

DECISIVE ACTION NEEDED

Although governments around the world now recognise the threat posed by global warming it has proved hard to get agreement on concerted action to deal with the problem. One of the first steps towards a global approach was the signing by most of the world's leaders of the United Nations Framework Convention on Climate Change in Rio de Janeiro in 1992. This committed the signatories to stabilise the levels of greenhouse gases emitted so as to prevent climate change.

The Kyoto Protocol is perhaps the best known of current international treaties. The United Nations organised an intergovernmental conference on climate change in Kyoto, Japan, in December 1997. The Protocol will be legally binding on signatory countries when signed by 55 countries (including sufficient developing countries to account for 55 per cent of developed world greenhouse gases). It requires developed countries to take action to reduce emissions of all six major greenhouse gases including ozone-depleting CFCs. On average, the developed world will reduce its greenhouse gases by over 5 per cent from the 1990 level by 2008–2012. The European Union is committed to achieving an 8 per cent reduction, whilst the United Kingdom agreed to a 12.5 per cent cut.

The treaty also encourages activities aimed at absorbing carbon such as tree planting. These create 'carbon sinks' that may be offset against a country's carbon account. Developed countries that exceed their Kyoto targets can sell their surplus to other countries that haven't achieved their targets. Countries can also fund greenhouse gas-reducing projects in other countries with the benefit in terms of emissions reduction going to the country funding the project.

Kyoto proposes other mechanisms, known as flexibility mechanisms (FM), that allow developed countries to gain credits to their carbon account. For example, the Clean Development Mechanism (CDM) allows developed world countries to enter into co-operative agreements to reduce emissions in the developing world. This might be achieved through the construction of an environmentally friendly power plant, for example. These projects may either reduce carbon dioxide emissions or increase the developing country's carbon sink.

The Kyoto Protocol has yet to come into effect. A follow-up meeting in The Hague in December 2000 failed to iron out problems with its implementation. Many of these relate to the difficulty in putting the flexibility mechanisms into place. While the concepts seem admirable, the difficulty lies in trying to develop rules that ensure that carbon dioxide levels reduce in total. In addition, there are concerns about the concept of the 'carbon sink' and what will be included or excluded in it.

Another difficult problem facing those attending The Hague meeting was how to establish penalties for non-compliance. The mechanism depends upon signatory countries honouring their agreement. It has little muscle to force those deviating from their targets to live up to their responsibilities. Difficulties may also arise if a country trades an apparent surplus only to find at a later stage that it has not met its own targets.

These and other complex issues are currently dogging the Kyoto Protocol. They suggest that the treaty will take time to ratify and probably without the United States at the start. However, it is more than likely that the United Kingdom and its European Union partners will ratify the treaty thus ensuring that the Kyoto Protocol impacts on our lives and business in this country in the future. It is hard to imagine that the United States will stay outside the process in the long term as US businesses are unlikely to forego the benefits of carbon dioxide trading, or to stay outside a new and potentially enormous carbon trading market.

DO INTERNATIONAL TREATIES ACHIEVE RESULTS?

There is some justification in questioning the effectiveness of international treaties or protocols. The world's governments became bogged down in acrimonious debate about how to put the Kyoto Protocol into practice in

The Hague in December 2000, and failed to move forward. The Bush administration has indicated that it is unlikely to sign up to Kyoto. This illustrates the difficulties in achieving agreement on specific measures acceptable to individual governments.

The experience of dealing with ozone depletion shows that concerted international effort is possible and that it can achieve results. The UNEP started addressing this issue in 1977. In 1985, the world's governments agreed to the Vienna Convention on the Protection of the Ozone Layer. Through this convention, governments committed themselves to protecting the ozone layer and to pooling scientific knowledge, all with the intention of building a better understanding of what was occurring in the stratosphere. It was through this co-operation that the global scientific community identified the chemicals partly responsible for the problem.

The Montreal Protocol on Substances That Deplete the Ozone Layer was adopted by governments in 1987 and has, to date, been further modified five times. Governments strengthened its provisions in London (1990), Copenhagen (1992), Vienna (1995), Montreal (1997) and Beijing (1999). This protocol aims to reduce and eventually eliminate the emissions of man-made ozone-depleting substances. It set limits on current usage and deadlines for the phasing out of the most significant chemicals (e.g., CFCs, carbon tetrachloride, methyl chloroform, HBFCs halons and methyl bromide). Production of the most damaging substances was eliminated (except for a few critical uses) by 1996 in developed countries, and will be eliminated by 2010 in developing countries.

The Montreal Protocol shows that governments can act together to achieve results. It also demonstrates that their decisions can have profound affects on businesses that happen to fall within the scope of such an initiative.

OTHER TREATIES THAT DEAL WITH SPECIFIC ENVIRONMENTAL ISSUES

There are close to 200 other international treaties, protocols and conventions concentrating on the environment and our interaction with it. These are generally referred to as multilateral environmental agreements (MEA). International regulation depends upon national sovereign governments agreeing to be bound by the regulation or law proposed. As a consequence, many international agreements are weak and woolly and difficult to turn into effective action. The two examples that follow highlight specific areas where governments have achieved agreement on proposals that have a useful outcome.

CITES, the Convention on International Trade in Endangered Species of Wild Fauna and Flora, came into force on 1 July, 1975 and now has a membership of 152 countries. This Convention aims to encourage the protection of endangered species through the regulation of trading in those species. The signatory governments act by banning commercial international trade in an agreed list of endangered species, and by regulating and monitoring trade in others that might become endangered. The control of whaling and the hunting of elephants for their ivory have been two issues that have brought this Convention to public attention. Smaller businesses involved in the import, export or re-export of exotic plants or animals must pay close attention to this Con-

vention and ensure that they do not transgress either UK laws or those in other countries through which they transport goods.

Governments have become increasingly concerned about the movement of waste across international borders and, in particular, the growth of an international trade in toxic waste for disposal. The 1986 Basle Convention on the Control of Transboundary Movements of Hazardous Wastes and Their Disposal aims to end the improper disposal of hazardous wastes and control their exportation. It is also concerned with the management and disposal of hazardous wastes at their source. The convention uses the concept of prior informed consent whereby anyone shipping waste must inform the appropriate authorities in the recipient state and obtain their consent.

WORLD TRADE AND THE ENVIRONMENT

International trade agreements have concentrated on liberalising trade and removing barriers to competition. Their success underpins the growth in international commerce. The two international instruments that have driven much of this change have been the General Agreement on Tariffs and Trade (GATT) and its successor, The World Trade Organisation (WTO).

Some argue that the continuing liberalisation of trade may be at the expense of the environment. A number of environmentalists object to WTO rules that both constrain the use of trade measures to extend domestic environmental standards beyond national borders and discriminate against imports that are believed to undermine domestic standards. The well-known tuna–dolphin dispute demonstrates environmentalists concerns. In 1991, the GATT ruled that US attempts to impose an import ban on tuna, aimed at preventing Mexican fishermen killing dolphins, was in contravention of the agreement on tariffs and trade. However, it appears that popular pressure will force governments in the developed world to strive to extend stricter environmental standards beyond their borders – using either pressure or inducements in other areas of economic activity as a lever.

There has been a shift in thinking about trade-related environmental issues. The Organisation for Economic Co-operation and Development (OECD) believes that greener public purchasing programmes are not necessarily a barrier to trade as long as they respect the fundamental underlying principles of free trade. Indeed, the OECD points out that a more liberal regime should help trade in environmental goods and services. The World Trade Organisation also recognises that environmental issues are of increasing importance in world trade. For example, it accepts that countries may act on imports to protect its own domestic environment (as long as they do not discriminate). In general, the WTO membership believes that an open, equitable and non-discriminatory multilateral trading system has a key contribution to make to national and international efforts to better protect environmental resources and promote sustainable development.

KEEPING TRACK OF INTERNATIONAL TREATIES

Unlike large corporations, SMEs cannot draw upon extensive internal research capabilities. Those in smaller companies charged with monitoring international developments in environmental regulations often have to combine this role with other responsibilities. The advent of the world-wide-web means that it is now possible for the smallest of SMEs to keep track of developments internationally. You will find useful information on websites run by the Department for the Environment, Food and Rural Affairs and the Department of Trade and Industry. The government sites will keep you up-to-date on proposed agreements and legislation. You should check these regularly. You should also examine the various international websites, such as that run by the United Nations Environment Programme, particularly relating to ozone and climate change, and others including CITES.

Exporters should explore the current regulations operating in their overseas markets. You should also make sure that you know what regulations apply in the countries that your products pass through in transit. Different governments treat transhipped goods in different ways. Even containerised goods are subject to local environmental regulations. Fortunately, UK and European Union regulations are among the most stringent so it should be relatively straightforward to adapt your product to comply with other countries requirements.

Business magazines such as *The Economist* have regular updates on developments in international trade. You will also find useful information on the global environment in libraries in third-level institutes.

APPROACHES TO REGULATION – THE BROAD PRINCIPLES

There are two distinct approaches taken to regulating the environment: command and control measures (CAC), and market-based instruments (MBI).

Command and control measures are the more traditional regulatory approach. These focus on enforcement measures and penalties and sanctions for any violations. Their benefits are that they are easy to put in place and generally straightforward and easy to understand. They often are the best and only route available to legislators dealing with acute, serious problems. Increasingly, though, regulators recognise that there are drawbacks associated with such regulations. Whilst the command aspect is straightforward, the control mechanisms can be cumbersome and difficult to operate. Agencies can find that their time is soaked up in ensuring compliance with, or prosecuting breaches of, the regulations rather than operating environmental protection programmes. There is a difficulty, too, where regulations set limits or bestow licences. Some companies may regard the limit as the acceptable level rather the maximum possible allowable. Perversely, regulations may encourage greater pollution, for example, than is possible using other mechanisms.

Accordingly, international bodies and governments are moving towards market-based instruments as a means of achieving environmental regulation. This approach attempts to shape the market so that industry and consumers favour the environmentally friendly route where a choice exists.

> Environmentally inspired fuel taxes or road charges are an example of the MBI approach. MBIs allow for greater flexibility and have the potential to do a lot more environmental good in the longer term.

> The energy labelling of washing machines and other white goods shows how MBIs can work in practice. These goods must carry a label showing the energy consumption and performance of the item with an overall rating on a seven-point scale where 'A' is the most efficient and 'G' is the least efficient. Consumers can choose the machine that they want, taking this additional information into account. Some purchasers will ignore it totally, whilst others will favour the environmentally friendly option once it is made clear to them. The hope is that consumers who might otherwise have chosen a 'G' machine may now select, for example, an 'F' instead. Thus, there will be a move up the scale. This positive shift will make producing environmentally friendly machines more cost-effective thus creating a continuing virtuous cycle.

The UK is one of the leaders in MBIs. Even still, the experience to date has been patchy as the Government grapples with the complexities of introducing mechanisms and dealing with the different interest groups involved in any specific measure. It is likely that these measures will become more common as the regulatory bodies develop experience in their development and administration.

THE PRINCIPLES UNDERPINNING ENVIRONMENTAL POLICIES

Modern environmental policies draw heavily upon a set of nationally and internationally accepted principles or goals. These are not laws in themselves and would be difficult to express fully in law. We discuss the main principles briefly here.

Sustainable development

The Earth Summit in Rio de Janeiro in June 1992 set the tone for much of the future development of environmental regulation. Officially titled 'The United Nations Conference on Environment and Development', the meeting was attended by representatives from 172 governments. It put in place a number of agreements and provided the foundation for further ones in the future. It also set in motion the process that led to the creation of a United Nations Commission for Sustainable Development (UNCSD). The meeting agreed an action plan for the twenty-first century that aims to bring about sustainable development. The action plan, known as 'Agenda 21', covers 13 core themes ranging from the atmosphere to biotechnology and radioactive waste. This is not binding on the signatory governments; instead, it is a programme for political and social action that aims to create a more environmentally friendly world.

Dr Gro Harlem Brundtland best defined sustainable development as being 'to meet the needs of the present without compromising the ability of future generations to meet their own needs.'[iv] Chris Patten quotes a friend who states this principle more simply as 'we should live on this earth as though we were intending to stay for good, not just for the weekend.' In many ways, the principle proposes a programme of continuous improvement. The concept of sustainable development, if adopted fully and rigorously pursued by a government, could have serious implications for any business. No government has, yet, done so.

The polluter pays principle (PPP)

This is one of the best-known environmental principles. It means that those who pollute should pay for the damage that they cause. This is based on the premise that no one should have a free lunch, and that those who pollute, especially businesses, should have to pay for their action. The European Union has adopted this principle explicitly in the Single European Act of 1987.

At face value this seems a laudable principle, but it can be difficult to put into practice. It is often hard to define the level of damage caused by an occurrence. For example, discharging warm water into a river does not necessarily kill fish or invertebrates. However, some animals will absorb toxins much faster in warmer water than in colder water and so may suffer as a consequence. The warm water discharge may have been the act that precipitated the damage, but it was not the sole cause.

Assessing the extent of any damage can be difficult. At present, we know so little about the environmental impact of most substances that our assessment of damage is at best an educated guess.

And there are the political consequences of applying the PPP. Rigorous application of this principle could close down factories unable to pay the true cost of the necessary clean-up. This raises the question as to whether it is justifiable to punish the employees of companies, especially if it is because of a one-off occurrence.

The preventative principle

This principle simply dictates that you should

avoid causing environmental damage rather than trying to make right the damage afterwards. The preventative principle underpins legislation and many good management practices. A simple example of the principle in practice is minimising waste by reducing product packaging. The preventative principle also makes good management sense on the grounds that prevention is better and cheaper than most cures.

The precautionary principle

The precautionary principle is highly controversial. The principle proposes controlling activities that may be harmful to health or the environment without conclusive evidence that they are so. This principle originated in Germany in the 1970s and 1980s. Since then, it has gained increasing political support internationally. It is enshrined in European Union and United Nations treaties as well as in national legislation.

The Rio Declaration of 1992 is an example of how the principle is presented. It states:

'In order to protect the environment, the precautionary approach shall be widely applied by States according to their capabilities. Where there are threats of serious irreversible damage, lack of full scientific certainty shall not be used as a reason for postponing cost-effective measures to prevent environmental degradation.'[v]

This statement demonstrates two important points about the precautionary principle:

1. it applies to serious risk

2. it applies where there is a lack of scientific agreement or knowledge about the risk involved.

The principle is controversial because some governments and other authorities feel that it has been used as an artificial trade barrier and that the vague nature of evidence required may encourage protectionism.

The European Commission has responded to criticism of the principle and its use of it by issuing a Communication clarifying its understanding of what it means. This Communication stresses that the Commission sees the principle as part of a structured approach to risk analysis. It sees it as applying:

'where scientific evidence is insufficient, inconclusive or uncertain and where preliminary scientific evaluation indicates that there are reasonable grounds for concern that the potentially dangerous effects on the environment, human, animal or plant health may be inconsistent with the high level of protection chosen by the EU.'[vi]

The Commission also stresses that the application of the precautionary principle should be transparent and, where possible, involve all interested parties. The Commission suggests that the precautionary principle should be:

- proportional to the required level of protection
- non-discriminatory in application
- consistent with similar measures already taken
- based on an examination of the potential benefits and costs of action or lack of action
- subject to review in the light of new scientific data

- capable of assigning responsibility for producing the scientific evidence necessary for a more comprehensive risk assessment.

WHAT YOU SHOULD DO

- Ensure that your business complies with the current international agreements.
- Link to the web and find out more about areas that may impact upon your business in the future.
- Identify any chemicals or business practices that may be regulated in the future (e.g., ozone-depleting chemicals) and start looking for alternatives.
- Exporters should track their products' routes and ensure that the products comply with the environmental regulations that apply not only in the destination market, but also in the countries that they pass through.
- Use your own buying power to make a difference by purchasing products that have a lower environmental impact.
- Look at your own business and try to establish what would happen if the environmental principles described in this chapter were to apply fully in your case.

NOTES TO CHAPTER 1

i   Burkino Faso, December 2000

ii   Intergovernmental Panel on Climate Change, IPCC, Working Group II, Summary for Policymakers, 2001

iii Department for the Environment, Transport and the Regions (November 2000), 'Climate Change: Draft UK Programme'.

iv Dr Gro Harlem Brundtland, cited by Chris Patten in 'Respect for the Earth' (Profile Books, 2000).

v   The Rio Declaration on Environment and Development 1992, The United Nations Conference on Environment and Development, Rio de Janeiro, June 1992.

vi European Commission, Communication on Precautionary Principle, Brussels, 2 February 2000.

CHAPTER 2

The European Union *and* environmental regulation

In this chapter, you'll find out:

- how the EU impacts on UK environmental legislation
- who does what in the EU
- how the EU develops and implements environmental regulations
- how these regulations impact upon SMEs
- what the main EU Regulations and Policy instruments are
- what the 6th Environmental Action Programme will mean for business
- what the European Environment Agency (EEA) does.

The European Union (EU) plays an important role in initiating and implementing environmental regulation across the member states including the United Kingdom. As the environmental impact of any activity does not necessarily respect national boundaries, so it is likely that the EU will take an even greater lead in proposing and establishing new environmental legislation for the member states. There are those who believe that the EU increases the quantity and reach of environmental legislation–increasing bureaucracy and making it harder to do business. However, European-wide legislation has the advantage of standardising regulation across borders and thus potentially reducing costs for compliant companies trading in a number of member states.

WHO DOES WHAT – THE EUROPEAN INSTITUTIONS

Originally, the EU focused on economic development. As its remit broadened, its institutions and treaties grew and developed. The EU has developed its own legal and regulatory structures to support this broadening of its role. The various treaties of the European Union are the primary source of EU law. There was no specific treaty basis for environmental measures until the Single European Act in 1987. This act broadened the original Treaty of Rome (1957, establishing the European Community) to allow environmental measures. The Maastricht Treaty (Treaty on European Union, TEU) in 1992 further strengthened this action by allowing more environmental legislation to be passed by a qualified majority rather than by unanimous decision.

Five institutions govern the development and implementation of the European Union's environmental policies and regulations. These are discussed, in turn, below.

The Council of Ministers

This is the EU's major decision-making body. It is made up of a single representative from each of the member states' governments. The presidency rotates every six months. Ministers attend the meetings dealing with their areas of responsibility. The General Secretariat and a Committee of Permanent Representatives of Member States (COREPER) prepare the agendas and manage the meetings.

The European Council

The heads of government and foreign ministers from the member states make up this body. It decides broad policy on the European Union's future at what are popularly called the Euro-Summits. These have become the focal point for demonstrations against, among other issues, damage to the environment.

The Commission

The Commission is like the European Union's civil service. The Commission consists of members (Commissioners) drawn from each of the member states with the larger nations, including the UK, having two. The President of the Commission is appointed unanimously by the member governments after consulting the European Parliament. The Commissioners do not represent their country, but are there to serve the interests of the entire European Union. The executive is divided into different Directorates-General (DGs) with a Commissioner heading each one. These are like ministries in national governments. While Directorate-General Environment (DG Environment) plays a major role in the EU's environmental regulation, other DGs are also involved.

The Commission is frequently criticised for being bureaucratic and unwieldy. (For example, DGs were known by a number written in Roman numerals rather than by a name reflecting their area of responsibility.) The Commission is attempting to change so that it is more transparent and responsive to European citizens. It now makes excellent use of the world-wide-web to disseminate information, and you can access most of its documentation easily through the respective websites of the different DGs.

The European Parliament

The European Parliament is not a law-making body like a national parliament. Its function is to advise and monitor other bodies and to comment upon proposed legislation. The EU has strengthened the Parliament's powers and it now has a co-decision-making role with the Council in areas relating to Monetary Union.

The voters in each member state directly elect the Members of the European Parliament (MEPs). This gives the Parliament significant moral authority in any debate. MEPs take an active interest in issues relating to the environment. A number of the current 626 MEPs are from Green parties and this representation helps to keep environmental issues to the fore. The MEPs exercise their greatest influence through the committee system in the Parliament. These committees examine legislation and then present recommendations for a vote of the full Parliament. There is one such committee for environmental matters.

The Court of Justice

This court fulfils two important functions. As an administrative court, it hears cases against member states and EU institutions. It also assesses the validity of EU legislation. In addition, the Court also acts as a constitutional court by providing definitive interpretations of EU law including the Treaties.

The court's judges come from the member states. The court has the power to find that a member state has failed to fulfil its obligations. The state then has to put in place measures that will ensure compliance.

HOW THE EUROPEAN UNION REGULATES

The European Union can regulate directly or through member state governments. The EU's authority comes from the treaties ratified by member states at different times. The treaties are akin to a constitution. There are three forms of EU legislation:

Regulations

An EU regulation is directly applicable, meaning that it automatically forms part of the law of a member state. Governments cannot change or amend a regulation once it has come into force and, as they come into force automatically, the individual member governments don't need to pass any legislation to bring the regulation into operation in their jurisdiction. Regulations impose uniformity across the EU. The Council of Ministers generally makes regulations.

Directives

Directives aim to achieve a common result throughout the EU. Their results are binding but member states can choose how they achieve that result. They are therefore not directly applicable. Member states decide what they need to do to put a directive into effect taking their own domestic circumstances and legislation into account. Either the Council of Ministers or the Commission issue directives.

Decisions

The Council of Ministers or the Commission make Decisions. These are addressed to specific entities such as a member state, companies, organisations or sometimes even individuals. Decisions are binding upon the entities involved.

THE EUROPEAN UNION'S ROLE IN ENVIRONMENTAL REGULATION

The European Union has taken an increasing interest in environmental issues since the early 1970s. Environmental disasters such as the Torry Canyon and an apparently constant decline in the quality of Europe's environment spurred the member states to action. The legal basis for the EU's environmental policy comes from articles 100a, 130r–130t of the Treaty on European Union. The amended Treaty of Rome allowed for EU measures that would:

- preserve, protect and improve the quality of the environment
- protect human health
- ensure a prudent and rational use of natural resources
- promote measures at an international level to deal with regional or worldwide environmental problems.

The EU has continued to add to and further define its environmental role. The Maastricht Treaty, properly known as the Treaty on European Union (TEU), states that the European Union will, among other things, promote balanced and sustainable economic progress. Further developments have strengthened the standing of environmental policy as an integral part of overall EU policy.

Environmental issues are now considered as part of the mainstream of the EU's overall activity. At a European Council meeting in Cardiff in 1998, the Council stressed that all programmes, especially those relating to energy, transport, and agriculture, should integrate the EU's environmental objectives into their operation. A subsequent meeting extended this to the internal market. All of this means that almost every EU programme, either policy or action, will take account of the environmental impact of that activity. This doesn't simply mean ensuring that it doesn't do any damage. The EU wants to see that all programmes contribute to the overall aim of balanced and sustainable development.

BIG IDEAS CAN HAVE A DIRECT IMPACT ON SMEs

For some people running small- and medium-sized enterprises it may seem that the broad and sometimes vague EU-wide policies are not immediately relevant to their business. However, here is an example of a policy direction that can have a direct and immediate impact on business.

The Commission has its headquarters in Brussels but has offices around the EU and beyond. It is a major purchaser of supplies and services for its own use. Increasingly, the Commission takes the environmental impact of each purchase into account. It uses recycled paper, low-energy lighting, non-toxic pens, recyclable equipment, environmentally friendly furniture, etc. This means that suppliers must meet these standards if they are to be successful in selling to the Commission.

It doesn't stop there. The EU wants to be sure that those providing services on its behalf also conform to the overall objectives of the EU's environmental policies. Suppliers can expect that the EU will insist on the best practical environmental practices from them in the future.

KEY INSTRUMENTS HELP ACHIEVE ENVIRONMENTAL GOALS

The European Union has moved away from the traditional command and control approach to a combination of measures aimed at delivering a better environment for European citizens. Important instruments in the EU's regulatory armoury include:

Environmental impact assessments

These are required to establish the extent of environmental impact of specific, usually large, projects. The impact assessments must allow public involvement.

Eco-labels

These labels identify products that are recognised as eco-friendly by the competent body in the member state. They allow consumers to take account of environmental impact in their purchasing decisions. Increasingly, too, the EU is insisting that household electrical goods carry an energy-usage label.

The Eco-audit programme

A voluntary scheme for companies in the European Union. Companies incorporate the appropriate environmental protection standards into their production processes and are audited under the aegis of the relevant agency in the member state.

Free access to information on environmental pollution

Free access to information on environmental pollution is ensured under a directive requiring national authorities to make environmental information available on request. The person enquiring does not have to prove that they have an interest in the information that they request.

The LIFE regulation

This regulation provides financial incentives for priority projects in the environmental field.

HOW IT ALL FITS TOGETHER

The Council of Ministers is the main driving force behind new environmental regulations and directives. The Council normally adopts new measures by a qualified majority but can choose to require unanimity in areas of fiscal policy, land use or energy supply.

The European Commission proposes legislation either as regulations or directives. It monitors the implementation of directives. Within the Commission, the Directorate-General Environment is responsible for the environment, nuclear safety and civil protection. The Commission develops its environmental proposals in line with a strategy set down in a multi-annual action programme. You can read more detail about the current programme later in this chapter.

The European Parliament's role varies depending on whether a decision is taken unanimously or by a qualified majority. The Council consults the Parliament where the issue requires unanimity but the Parliament's opinions are not binding. The Parliament may propose amendments to Council decisions made by the qualified majority.

The European Committee on the Environment, Public Health and Consumer Protection deals with environmental issues in the Parliament.

THE MAIN EUROPEAN LEGISLATION

The EU has produced a wide range of legislation relating to the environment and environmental issues as follows:

Water

The EU has issued a number of directives aimed at protecting surface and underground water supplies. These set quality standards for drinking and bathing water, as well as water for fish and shellfish rearing. They control the discharge of toxins.

Air and the atmosphere

These directives aim to control pollution from large combustion plants and the emissions from motor vehicles. The EU has also acted to phase out substances implicated in the destruction of the ozone layer. One measure currently under consideration is the proposed carbon tax to be levied on fuels such as oil or coal.

Noise

Directives under this heading set the maximum allowable levels for noise pollution from vehicles, aircraft, and a range of other outdoor equipment. Manufacturers or distributors must give information on the noise levels emanating from household appliances on their packaging.

Chemicals

There is a European inventory of all chemical products available setting out the procedures for notification, evaluation and control. Directives control the packaging, distribution and use of dangerous chemicals and govern the composition of detergents. Another directive requires that manufacturers inform the relevant authorities about certain substances, where they are manufactured and the possible location of accidents.

Waste

The EU has established a body of legislation relating to the reduction, recycling, disposal and processing of waste. The EU has also addressed the movement of wastes across national borders.

Nature conservation and protection

Directives under this heading cover the conservation of important habitats and areas of special interest. They ban the importation of certain products, for example, those made from baby seal fur, and they control and restrict scientific experiments on animals.

THE EU ENVIRONMENT ACTION PROGRAMMES

The European Union has operated action programmes on the environment since 1973. The initial programmes ran for between five and seven years. The programmes aimed to stimulate and support action in certain key areas and move the EU towards better environmental management. In the early stages, the programmes focused on pollution control and prevention.

The emphasis changed as the EU's programmes developed. The EU now places a greater stress on integrating environmental policy into agricultural, industrial and social policy. The programmes moved from the view that good environmental management was of necessity an extra cost to the view that good environmental management was also good business and economic management in the long term. Increasingly, the programmes have become more proactive and focus on dealing with environmental issues before they result in environmental damage.

The global assessment of the fifth Environment Action Programme (1992–1999) concluded that whilst it had contributed to progress in some areas, problems remained and the environment will continue to deteriorate unless:

- greater progress is made in the implementation of legislation in member states
- environmental policies are integrated further into the environmental and social programmes that give rise to the environmental pressures in the first place
- stakeholders and citizens take more ownership of efforts to protect the environment
- there are new measures introduced to address serious and persistent current and emerging environmental problems.

The main thrust of these findings is that there is insufficient legislation and that member states are not implementing current legislation quickly or enthusiastically enough. The assessment sees a need for more emphasis on market-based and consumer initiatives. For business, this will mean more legislation coupled with better enforcement. It will also result in customers favouring more environmentally friendly options when making their purchasing decisions.

NEW PROGRAMME SETS TARGETS WITH SIGNIFICANT BUSINESS IMPLICATIONS

The sixth Environment Action Programme, entitled 'Environment 2010 Our Future, Our Choice',[ii] proposes action on the areas identified in the global assessment of the previous, fifth programme. The programme runs for between five and ten years from 2001.

The programme is ambitious, with its broad aims being to:

- tackle climate change
- protect nature and wildlife
- address environment and health issues
- preserve natural resources and manage waste.

At first glance, these aims may seem of little direct or immediate concern to SMEs. However, the programme's details show that it has the potential to affect every business, large or small, and it could have major implications for some sectors and businesses.

Climate change

In its summary document, the Commission states that its objective in relation to climate change is to 'stabilise concentrations of greenhouse gases in the atmosphere at a level that will not cause unnatural variations in the Earth's climate'.

The programme identifies what needs to be done to achieve this, including the reduction of greenhouse gas emissions by 8 per cent, compared with the 1990 baseline, by 2008–2012. In the longer term, the aim will be to reduce these further, by approximately 20–40 per cent by 2020 with a 70 per cent reduction as the ultimate target.

Some of the likely consequences of this will be:

- an accelerated shift towards renewable energy sources
- establishment of a greenhouse gas emissions trading scheme
- introduction and increases in carbon taxes
- more favourable treatment for companies that reduce greenhouse gases significantly.

This will create opportunities for some sectors and businesses while increasing the cost-base for others. For example, parts sub-suppliers to the traditional generating industries may need to start building links with renewable energy producers – and developing products that meet their needs. Businesses heavily dependent on road freight might be well-advised to examine alternative transportation options.

Nature and wildlife

In protecting nature and wildlife, the programme focuses on: restoring the structure and functioning of natural systems, halving the loss of biodiversity both in the EU and on a global scale, and protecting soil against erosion and pollution. If implemented, this will have implications for certain business sectors. Companies may have to bear increased remediation costs and it is likely that planning regulations will become even stricter.

Health and the environment

This objective aims to deliver an environment of such quality that the levels of man-made contaminants do not give rise to significant impacts on, or risks to, human health. This objective recognises the benefits that we derive from the 30,000 synthetic chemicals used in the European Union. There are already strict standards and regulations in place governing their use. This action focuses, in the first instance, on assessing and reducing their impact on human health whilst managing their use.

The areas singled out for mention in the action programme under this heading are: agricultural pesticides, water (particularly in towns and cities), air pollution, noise and its impact on human health.

Most of the actions proposed under this heading aim to improve our knowledge and information about certain risks. One specific point proposed is the requirement that local authorities create 'noise maps' and set noise objectives when they make planning decisions.

Natural resources and waste

The objective under this heading is to shift the emphasis towards waste prevention, followed by recycling, waste recovery and incineration, and finally, only as a last resort, land-fill. The target figures are to reduce the quantity of waste going to final disposal by around 20 per cent on 2000 levels by 2010, and 50 per cent by 2050.

This action will:

- make producers responsible for the collecting, treating and recycling of their waste products
- encourage consumers to select products and services that create less waste
- develop and promote a European Union-wide strategy on waste recycling, with targets and monitoring to allow member states to compare progress
- promote the development of a market for recycled materials
- develop specific actions, under an Integrated Product Policy approach, to promote the greening of products and processes. By way of example, the Commission quotes the concept of intelligent product design that reduces the environmental impacts of products from their conception to the end of their useful life.

WORKING ACROSS THE EUROPEAN UNION

One of the important elements of this programme is the intention to ensure that the programme has an impact across all areas of the European Union. The programme plans to speed up the development and implementation of European environmental regulations. It aims to adopt a 'name and shame' approach to those national governments that don't implement EU laws as quickly as they should. The programme will also put the environment at the heart of all EU actions. This means that the EU will expect the Commission, national governments and local authorities to address and tackle environmental issues through all of their policies, and not just environmental ones.

In addition, the EU plans to make more effective use of market-based instruments to encourage more environmentally friendly products and services and greater compliance with environmental regulations. The programme sees significant 'green growth' opportunities for business. Purchases by public bodies make up 14 per cent of the European market. The programme envisages making this a greener market segment with government and state bodies favouring green products.

The programme will also target the financial sector and encourage it to make more environmentally friendly investments and to encourage greener financial reporting. Coupled with this, the programme envisages greater consumer information and action aimed at encouraging environmentally friendly choices.

WINNERS AND LOSERS

The action programme creates a range of business opportunities and will also affect some current business operations.

Some business winners:

- solar heater producers
- insulation manufacturers
- producers of efficient boilers
- producers physically near to their market (lower transport costs)
- lower energy manufacturers
- businesses using alternative energy sources
- eco-tour organisers
- recycling companies
- forestry developers
- aquaculture
- remediation providers
- producers of beach and other environmental protection
- organic fertiliser producers
- organic farmers
- suppliers of environmentally friendly office – and other supplies.

The likely losers include:

- traditional energy producers and sub-suppliers to the traditional energy sector
- those with a high dependency on road-based transport
- companies with contaminated lands
- those using materials from environmentally sensitive areas
- traditional fertiliser and pesticide producers
- intensive farmers
- the traditional fishing sector

- traditional chemical producers and users
- transportation companies
- waste-intensive processes
- producers of high energy-using appliances.

THE EU ENVIRONMENT AGENCY

The Council of Ministers adopted a regulation in 1990 allowing for the formation of the European Environment Agency. Three years later, they decided that this should be based in Copenhagen. The agency has a staff of approximately 70 and a budget approaching Euro 20 million.

The purpose of the EEA is to supply member states with up-to-date, comparative information. The agency sees its role as supporting policy preparation and implementation through effective information collection and interpretation systems.

The agency is mandated to fulfil a wide range of functions which, in practice, cover the three main areas of networking, monitoring and reporting, as well as acting as a reference centre. The EEA is developing the European Environmental Information and Observation Network (EIONET) to allow for European-wide environmental data collection and processing.

The EEA's activities are organised into five programme areas:

1. topic databases and reporting
2. integrated assessment
3. periodical reporting
4. reporting system support
5. service network and infrastructure.

It will give priority to:

- waste
- air emissions
- noise pollution
- environmentally hazardous chemicals
- water resources
- soil, flora and fauna
- coastal protection.

Although a relatively young organisation, it is very likely that the EEA will play an increasingly important role in the harmonisation and standardisation of environmental data. This information will guide both EU legislation and its enforcement. The EEA will also play an important advisory and monitoring role across a range of environmental policies and initiatives.

WHAT YOU NEED TO KNOW AND DO

It's difficult to keep track of the range of environmental programmes and legislation in the European Union. At a very minimum, companies should check the EU environmental website regularly and keep up to date with what's going on in the Environmental DG. They should ensure that they are on the DG's mailing lists and that they receive the regular EU newsletters produced in both printed and e-mail form.

SME's are unlikely to be able to affect proposed legislation on their own, but they should be aware of it and where necessary join with others in lobbying the Commission and more importantly their local MEP (Member of the European Parliament).

You should follow the progress of legislation through the EU and take part in the consultation process at the DEFRA stage. Don't wait for EU legislation to be converted to UK legislation before taking action. Try to ensure that your business plans will comply with potential EU regulations.

If you supply environmentally friendly products, you should make sure that you can prove your environmental credentials and consider competing for EU tenders.

NOTES TO CHAPTER 2

i   Life: Regulation (EEC) No 1973/92 of 21 May 1992 (Official Journal No L 206 of 22 July 1992) as modified by Regulation (EC) No 1404/96 of 15 July 1996 (Official Journal No L 181 of 20 July 1996).

ii   6th Environment Action Programme, 'Environment 2010 Our Future, Our Choice', Commission of the European Union (2000).

CHAPTER 3

Your business *and* environmental law

In this chapter, we explain:

- the basic legal framework
- how legislation comes into existence
- the main environmental legislation
- your liability and how you might break the law.

Obviously, the law is very important in environmental regulation. At its worst, if your company falls foul of the courts, you could face imprisonment or heavy fines. The courts now take environmental matters seriously and are willing and empowered to act against companies that fail to live up to their environmental obligations.

This chapter examines the law relating to the environment, and it covers the main legal issues you may face. It explains some of the important legal concepts underlying our laws and tells you how legislation comes into being at national level. It lists the different types of legislation and some of the key terms used in the UK. It also points you to where you can find out more about specific legal areas.

THE LEGAL FRAMEWORK

It is essential that business personnel understand the legal framework underpinning environmental law. Unlike its fellow members of the European Union, the UK does not have a written constitution. Instead, it depends upon three legal pillars to support its legal system:

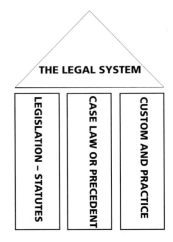

THE LEGAL SYSTEM

LEGISLATION – STATUTES

CASE LAW OR PRECEDENT

CUSTOM AND PRACTICE

'Custom and practice' refers to rules based upon social or commercial custom. Once accepted by the courts, custom and practice is binding in law. Custom and practice operates in areas that are not covered by specific legislation and it must be possible to demonstrate that something has been custom and practice for a period of time.

'Case law and precedent' reflects the need for fairness and standardisation in court decisions. The doctrine of *stare rationibus decidendis* requires that a later court applies the same rationale as an earlier court where both cases involve the same essential issues. Courts interpret legislation, both national and European, or apply common law and thus build up a huge case law structure.

LEGISLATION

There are two sources of legislation in the UK: Parliament and the European Union. Under English law, Parliament is sovereign. An Act of Parliament is therefore the highest form of law. Judges may have to interpret legislation passed if it is ambiguous in some way.

THE ENVIRONMENT – YOUR LEGAL DUTIES

Like everyone else, people running a business have to obey the law. The business too, as a legal entity, has to do the same. Environmental legislation has grown up in a higgledy-piggledy way over the centuries. This has been in response to what people saw as important at different times. This isn't very helpful for business. Indeed, it would have been much simpler if, at some time before the industrial revolution, a government had had the foresight to establish legislation that covered

all aspects of business's interaction with its surrounding environment. Instead, laws and legal practice developed mainly in response to problems rather than in advance of them. Sometimes regulations, developed for one situation, have been applied in a completely different context.

We can divide legal regulation into two types:

1. Specific environmental laws or regulations are developed to manage and protect the environment. These are normally enacted by Parliament or the European Union and are generally clearer and more specific than other general law.

2. General laws or regulations are controls that are broadly applied and can include environmental issues. These often stem from common law, case law or precedent. A typical example of this is the legal concept of nuisance. For SMEs these general regulations are more difficult to monitor and manage as they are broader and often more wide ranging. As each case is decided on its own merits, it can be difficult to know in advance what is or isn't allowable under the more general legal framework.

There are certain legal concepts that you should understand to ensure that you are not breaking the law or putting your business at risk, and we address some of these in the following pages. Ignorance is no excuse in law and so you should take a critical look at your business and see if there are possible areas or activities that may be inadvertently transgressing the law or someone's rights.

HOW ENVIRONMENTAL LAWS COME INTO BEING

The Government is the normal source of new legislation. A number of different organisations or groups may suggest the need for legislation. These include statutory agencies such as the Environment Agency or non-governmental bodies such as Friends of the Earth. The Government may also introduce legislation to put a European Union directive into force or to meet commitments under an international treaty such as CITES. Sometimes the courts may prompt the Government into action. Individual MPs, too, have a certain amount of time available to introduce new legislation.

THE CONSULTATION PROCESS – SHAPING LEGISLATION

The Government engages in a consultation process once it has proposed legislation. It may issue either a Green or White Paper. The Green Paper gives an outline or tentative proposals for discussion while the White Paper describes firm policy.

The consultation process is an important step in the development of legislation. The Government's aim is to produce effective legislation taking the views of interested parties into account. There may be several stages in the consultation process. Typically, the appropriate Department will post its initial consultation document on its website. It then invites those interested to submit their views on the topic. The Department for Environment, Food & Rural Affairs, the Department of Trade and Industry, the Health and Safety Commission are the main sources of proposed environmental legislation. Departments will post the consultative documents at their various stages of development on their websites.

WHAT YOU SHOULD DO

Companies should monitor what legislation is proposed or in train and assess its likely implications for their businesses. Proposed legislation can change radically during this consultative process so it is essential that companies track the progress through the system.

If you feel that your interests are affected by the suggested legislation, you should consider making a submission directly to the appropriate Ministry. Another, and possibly more effective, way of having an impact is through representative organisations such as the Confederation of British Industry. There is a wide range of representative and sectoral organisations. You should make sure that you are a member of your appropriate bodies and that you pay special attention to any notification about proposed legislation. It's much harder to change legislation once it has gone through the drafting process.

There are further opportunities to amend potential legislation after it has been drafted by civil servants. The Bill has first and second readings before entering the committee stage. The committee stage is where the Bill is discussed point-by-point. A standing committee usually does this, but sometimes the whole House discusses major issues at this juncture. The committee stage may amend the Bill. Again, you should pay close attention to the progress of legislation through the committee stage as it can change significantly.

You may have been happy with the draft document, but then discover that the final legislation has changed and now has a greater, possibly less favourable, impact on your business. Remember that larger businesses will lobby extensively to protect their interests. SMEs are generally more flexible and adaptable. Some proposed changes will give smaller companies a competitive advantage over their larger rivals. Multinationals are unlikely to allow this to happen without putting up a fight. Be ready, therefore, to lobby on your own behalf if the business opportunity is worth it.

The House discusses the Bill further at the report stage when the committee stage and other amendments are voted upon. The Bill then goes through a third reading and then progresses to the House of Lords to repeat this process.

HOW SCOTLAND AND NORTHERN IRELAND DIFFER

Both Scotland and Northern Ireland have a Secretary of State of cabinet rank supported by junior ministers. Each administration has its own individual ministries responsible, in part, for environmental concerns in their area. The Lord Advocate and the Solicitor General in Scotland are both Crown Ministers separate from the Secretary of State.

Scotland's legal system differs in certain significant respects to that of England and Wales. This difference is beyond the scope of this publication. Devolution to Scotland, Northern Ireland and Wales is also resulting in distinct approaches to environmental regulation in tune with the broader differences between the regions. However, as much

modern environmental legislation stems from EU agreements and common policies, the result is generally the same regardless of the jurisdiction.

THE MAIN ENVIRONMENTAL ACTS AFFECTING BUSINESSES

We list the main environmental legislation below in chronological order, starting from the Control of Pollution Act 1974. It is important to note that later legislation often amends or even repeals earlier laws. You should view any piece of legislation in the context of all of the legislation passed. Later in this section, we offer some advice on how to keep up to date with legal developments. In Chapters 5 and 6, we go into greater depth about legislation affecting SMEs.

Control of Pollution Act 1974/ Control of Pollution Amendment Act 1989

This is a key early Act dealing with waste disposal, water pollution, noise, atmospheric pollution and public health, subsequently revised by the amending legislation.

Environmental Protection Act 1990

An important Act that not only builds on previous Acts such as the Control of Pollution Act, but develops a much more integrated approach to pollution control. The Government has modified and expanded upon this Act several times since. Those with a serious interest in environmental legislation should read this Act in full.

Part I of this Act contains the Integrated Pollution Control (IPC) and the Local Air

Pollution Control (LAPC) regimes. Central to both these regimes is the requirement that the 'Best Available Techniques Not Entailing Excessive Costs' (BATNEEC) should be used to prevent or minimise pollution. This is designed to provide a flexible, case-by-case approach to regulation balancing cost with environmental benefit.

Water Industry Act 1991

This Act deals with the supply of water and the provision of sewage services. It covers effluent discharge into the sewage system and special category effluent.

Water Resources Act 1991

This Act consolidated enactments relating to the National Rivers Authority and its functions. It deals with the classification of water quality, water pollution control, abandoned mines, pollution control registers, and the liabilities of directors and others.

Clean Air Act 1993

This updated the Clean Air Acts of 1956 and 1968. As its name implies, it tackles issues relating to smoke, grit, dust and fume emissions. It also regulates motor fuel from the perspective of the pollution caused by its composition.

Noise and Statutory Nuisance Act 1993

Certain street noise becomes a statutory nuisance under this Act. This Act governs the use of loudspeakers and audible intruder alarms. It sets out the role of local authorities and allows them to recover costs by making a charge on the premises to which they relate.

Environment Act 1995

This establishes the Environment Agency and the Scottish Environment Protection Agency. It sets out their roles and transfers the functions of the National Rivers Authority. It amends previous legislation to provide for the new Agencies. It is a comprehensive Act and covers most areas of environmental control. It defines the relationship with the local authorities.

Noise Act 1996

The Act covers noise coming from dwellings at night and allows for the forfeiture and confiscation of equipment used to make noise unlawfully.

Pollution Prevention and Control Act 1999

The European Council Directive on Integrated Pollution Prevention and Control requires that a range of industrial installations are regulated by a system of integrated pollution control. This is a system that looks at the entire impact of an installation on the environment. It takes air, water, land and other environmental impacts together and sets conditions to deliver a high level of environmental protection. The Pollution Prevention and Control Act gives effect to this directive in the UK. Businesses will now receive permits based on the concept of 'Best Available Technology' which is a very similar concept to BATNEEC described under the Environment Protection Act of 1990. Many of the businesses are already regulated under the Environmental Protection Act 1990; however, the 1999 Act now covers large, intensive pig and poultry installations, plus large food and drink manufacturing installations.

DELEGATED LEGISLATION – SIGNIFICANT IN RELATION TO THE ENVIRONMENT

Parliament has the power to, and frequently does, delegate legislative power to certain bodies and individuals. Parliament normally grants these powers in an Enabling Act. This Act defines the powers of the delegated legislator. There are differences between delegated legislation and primary legislation: you cannot challenge primary legislation in the courts, whilst delegated legislation is subject to judicial review.

Ministers can make rules, regulations and orders. These delegated powers are known as statutory instruments (SIs). They operate nationally and allow the Minister to deal with complex and technical issues.

This is especially important in environmental legislation where delegated powers are commonplace. When dealing with emission limits for prescribed substances in the Environmental Protection Act of 1990, the Act states that:

The Secretary of State may make regulations under subsection (2) or (4) below establishing standards, objectives or requirements in relation to particular prescribed processes or particular substances.

The Environmental Protection Act delegates significant powers to the Minister, as does most legislation in the environmental field. This procedure helps to keep the overall Act simple and straightforward. It also allows the Minister to keep the regulations up to date and to take new scientific information and developments into account.

It is important that companies keep abreast of developments in both primary legislation and subsequent regulations. It is likely that the regulations will be of equal significance for SMEs.

There are more statutory instruments than Acts. You will find details of these on the HMSO website or from the relevant government department.

Byelaws are a form of delegated legislation

Local authorities generally issue byelaws. These are local in effect and only apply where the authority has jurisdiction. Some state corporations also have the power to issue byelaws.

WHAT ABOUT COMMON LAW?

Common law represents the very earliest form of law offered through the court system. It was originally based on the assumption that the law as administered by the King's courts represented the common custom of the realm. The term common law now refers to laws or customs that have been recognised as law by judges ruling on particular cases. The distinctive feature of the common law is that it represents the law as expressed in judicial decisions. The grounds for deciding on a particular case are found in precedents set in past decisions. This body of law has grown up since Norman times and is an important element of environmental regulation.

TORT

Tort refers to any wrong, other than breach of contract, for which there is a remedy either through damages or by compensation.

NUISANCE AND THE ENVIRONMENT – AN IMPORTANT ISSUE FOR MANAGERS

The concept of nuisance is most important from an environmental perspective. We usually identify three types of nuisance:

1. Private nuisance affects one or a small number of individuals. Those alleging that they have been wronged must take a civil action and seek redress in the civil courts.

2. Public nuisance is defined as any nuisance that materially affects the reasonable comfort and convenience of the life of Her Majesty's subjects. It occurs where the nuisance materially affects the general public or one specific group. This is a tort and a criminal offence and is normally prosecuted by the authorities – either the Attorney General or the police.

3. Statutory nuisance: In a number of cases, laws now govern activities that would formerly have been treated as private nuisance. Local authorities now have wide-ranging powers relating to environmental nuisances under legislation such as the Public Health Act 1936 and the Control of Pollution Act 1974.

EARLY CASE SHOWS HOW NUISANCE CAN AFFECT BUSINESS

In an early case of its kind, St Helens Smelting Co Ltd versus Tipping, a landowner took out an action against a mining company. He bought an estate close to the copper-smelting plant in June 1860. The works increased production in September of the same year. As a consequence of the increase in pollution, the vegetation in the estate suffered damage. The court had to balance the right to enjoy property with the right to conduct a business.

This case went all of the way to the House of Lords. The Lords found in favour of the estate owner because actual, physical damage had been done to his property. The pollution was therefore a nuisance. The Lords distinguished between the nuisance that caused damage to property and nuisance that interfered with the use and enjoyment of the property.

Private nuisance – important but limited

Private nuisance, while important, is limited in its applicability to environmental problems for the following reasons:

- It must involve property and the person taking the action must have an interest in that property.
- An individual must take the action against the alleged body causing the nuisance. This requires time and resources.
- The court cannot take other wider interests into account. The courts are careful to deal with the specific case and do not establish uniform standards for all occasions.

There are other factors that influence nuisance including the character of the neighbourhood, the timing and the duration of the alleged nuisance, the level of comfort and reasonableness of the antagonists.

Individuals have three basic remedies for nuisance: abatement, damages and injunctions. Abatement means that the individual stops the nuisance directly. This, although legal, is generally ill advised as the person taking such action could face prosecution themselves for damage that they cause or simply trespassing on another's property.

Nuisance is treated differently in Scotland. The Scottish courts don't distinguish between private and public nuisance, nor do they need evidence of physical damage. The courts can accept serious disturbance or exposure of people or their property to the risk of damage as grounds for nuisance.

Pigeons, business and nuisance

Nuisance does not always imply that the person prosecuted is either directly responsible or aware of the problem. An interesting case, Wandsworth Borough Council versus Railtrack plc, shows that a landowner, in this case Railtrack, can be prosecuted for a nuisance emanating from his land even though he does not create the nuisance nor does he do anything to encourage or sustain it. Pigeons roosting on a Railtrack bridge were deemed to be causing a nuisance to people passing underneath. The birds were regular, run of the mill, street pigeons and were not employed by Railtrack as couriers or in any other position. Railtrack was found to be liable for the correction of this nuisance.

NEGLIGENCE AND YOUR DUTY OF CARE

You or your business are negligent if you don't take proper care where you have a duty to do so and where as a consequence of that failure the person to whom you owe the duty suffers loss or damage. This amounts to more than simply being careless as there has to be proof that damage occurred. The tort of negligence requires that you take reasonable care to avoid acts or omissions that you can reasonably see might cause injury to your neighbour. In negligence cases, your neighbour is someone so closely and directly affected by your action that you realised that they would be affected when you considered taking the action in the first place.

However, people are not liable for every negligent act that they might commit. Negligence is limited by the requirement that the defendant owes those claiming against him or her a duty of care. Legislation can also set out a duty of care. For example, the Environmental Protection Act 1990 obliges you to take all reasonable steps to keep waste safe. It extends this duty of care to whoever you authorise to take it from you. This duty of care applies to anyone who produces, imports, keeps, stores, transports, treats or disposes of waste. It also applies to anyone acting as a broker or agent who arranges any of the above.

CAN MY COMPANY BE PROSECUTED?

Many SMEs are limited liability companies. The law treats these as entities in their own right and separate from their owners, board, directors and employees. Generally, the company is held liable for any breaches of environmental laws such as the Environmental Protection Act. However, there are circumstances where individuals and employees may be liable to prosecution.

Those people running businesses without the protection of limited liability may find themselves directly liable to fines or even imprisonment for offences under the environmental laws. The Environmental Protection Act (1990, amended in the 1995 Act) states that a person guilty of certain offences may be liable:

(a) on summary conviction, to a fine not exceeding £20,000 or imprisonment for a term not exceeding three months, or both;

(b) on conviction in indictment to a fine or to imprisonment for a term not exceeding two years, or both.

The courts are willing to act against those offending against the environmental laws and will use fines and imprisonment as appropriate.

AM I PERSONALLY PROTECTED BY LIMITED LIABILITY?

Some company managers and directors believe that limited liability protects them personally from prosecution under the various environmental laws. This is not the case. Directors, managers, company secretaries or others may be prosecuted where they are viewed to have been neglectful or contributed knowingly to the problem. The Environmental Protection Act 1990 states in section 157:

(1) Where an offence under any provision of this Act committed by a body corporate is proved to have been committed with the consent or connivance of, or to have been attributable to any neglect on the part of, any director, manager, secretary or other similar officer of the body corporate or a person who was purporting to act in any such capacity, he as well as the body corporate shall be guilty of that offence and shall be liable to be proceeded against and punished accordingly.

(2) Where the affairs of a body corporate are managed by its members, subsection (1) above shall apply in relation to the acts or defaults of a member in connection with his functions of management as if he were a director of the body corporate.

WHAT IF I'M A SUB-SUPPLIER?

The Environmental Protection Act is even broader in its scope than simply focusing on those working in the company judged to have committed the offence. It also states that:

Where the commission by any person of an offence (as defined in the Act) ... is due to the act or default of some other person, that other person may be charged and convicted of the offence by virtue of this section whether or not proceedings for the offence are taken against the first-mentioned person.

This shows that even those who do not work for the company may be prosecuted if they are considered to have contributed in some way to the offence. This is important for sub-suppliers who may assume that their larger customers are responsible as they produce the end-product. This legislation clearly means that every company or individual in the business chain must be aware of, and fully comply with, the appropriate environmental legislation.

HOW DO I KEEP UP WITH ALL OF THIS STUFF?

It's hard enough to manage the day-to-day operations without having to watch what's happening in Parliament or the corridors and offices of the various ministries. However, you should:

- Get copies of the legislation and regulations that affect your business and keep this collection up to date by regularly checking for amendments and new regulations. The HMSO website or other annual publications contain this material.

- Check the DEFRA and DTI websites regularly and find out what is under consideration.

- Join your representative business associations, particularly sectoral ones, and ask to be kept up to date on changes in environmental regulations.

- Write to your local MP and councillors and give them information about your company. Request that they keep you informed of issues of concern to your sector that may be considered in Parliament or your local council.

- Subscribe to an environmental legislative monitoring service and receive regular updates on changes and developments in the area.

CHAPTER 4

Who does what – a guide through the regulatory maze

This chapter gives an overview of the main government bodies involved in environmental regulation in the UK. It explains the role of the Department for Environment, Food & Rural Affairs (DEFRA). It looks at the some of the bodies under its aegis, including the Environment Agency. It describes the environmental activities of the Department for Trade and Industry (DTI), the Scottish Environmental Protection Agency (SEPA), the Northern Ireland Environment and Heritage Service, and local authorities.

The Government is the main source of regulation in the UK. It emphasises the importance of the environment in its thinking and policies. Its environmental strategy is built upon four key pillars:

1. identifying problems and risks
2. setting objectives and targets where appropriate
3. appraising, selecting, consulting and implementing the most appropriate set of policy instruments (such as taxes, charges, permit trading, regulation, public spending or voluntary agreements) for the circumstances
4. evaluating the success of policies, modifying them where appropriate and applying experience from one area of policy to another.

A number of Government departments play a central role in putting this strategy in to practice, with the most important of these being the Department for the Environment, Food & Rural Affairs. As we write, the departments are implementing a major re-organisation of responsibilities. The following is based on the best information available at the time of writing and may change as departments settle into their new roles.

DEFRA – AT THE CENTRE OF ENVIRONMENTAL REGULATION AND PLANNING

DEFRA shapes and directs the major proportion of the UK's policy and regulation specifically relating to the environment. It operates at an international level in negotiating and helping develop worldwide and European treaties, policies and regulations. It prepares national legislation through its agencies and the local authorities.

The Department was created after the June 2001 general election and brought together:

- The Environment Protection Group from the former Department of the Environment, Transport and the Regions (DETR)
- The Wildlife and Countryside Directorate, also from DETR
- The functions of the former Ministry of Agriculture, Fisheries & Food (MAFF)
- Responsibility for certain animal welfare issues and hunting formerly handled by the Home Office.

The Department's overall aims are to improve everyone's quality of life, now and for the future, through:

- a better environment
- thriving rural economies and communities
- diversity and abundance of wildlife resources
- a countryside for all to enjoy

- sustainable and diverse farming and food industries that work together to meet the needs of consumers.

WHAT DEFRA AIMS TO DO

DEFRA has set out what it wants to achieve. These key tasks will establish the agenda for future legislation and regulation. The Department aims to achieve the following in relation to the environment:

- Position DEFRA as the leading voice in Government for sustainable development, environmental protection and the renewal of rural areas, and secure the trust and support of partners and stakeholders.
- Protect and improve the environment and integrate the environment with other policies across Government and internationally.
- Play a leading role in seeking international agreement on climate change, and implement the UK's own programme to meet its target.
- Promote less wasteful use of natural resources (energy, waste, water, etc.) both in the UK and worldwide.
- Conserve and enhance the diversity and abundance of English wildlife and protect globally threatened animals and plants.
- Set the future direction for the rural economy, food and farming.

DEFRA sponsors a number of important non-departmental public bodies (NDPBs) including:

- the Environment Agency
- the Countryside Agency
- English Nature
- Royal Commission on Environmental Pollution.

Executive agencies deliver most of the Department's direct services. In addition to those listed above, DEFRA also sponsors a range of other committees and NDPBs, including:

- the Advisory Committee on Business and the Environment
- the Government Panel on Sustainable Development
- Expert Panel on Air Quality Standards
- the UK Round Table on Sustainable Development.

Environmental protection is a key area of interest for the DEFRA. The environmental group in the Department deals with issues such as:

- air quality
- chemicals and biotechnology
- climate change
- energy efficiency and fuel poverty
- contaminated land and environmental liability
- noise and nuisance
- pollution prevention and control
- radioactivity – discharges and waste
- waste and recycling
- water.

DEFRA supplies the secretariat for a range of groups and committees working on key environmental tasks.

THE ENVIRONMENT AGENCY

The Environment Agency is the largest NDPB supported by DEFRA. It has funding of approximately £585 million, 75 per cent of which comes from their own charges with DEFRA providing the remainder. It has a staff of approximately 10,000. The vast majority of these work in the Agency's 26 area offices. In addition, the Agency has seven regional offices and an office in Cardiff representing Environment Agency Wales.

The Environment Act of 1995 established the Environment Agency. In addition to the duties assigned to it in that Act, it also took over functions from bodies such as the National Rivers Authority. It is responsible for an area of approximately 15 million hectares (37 million acres) of land, 36,000 km (22,000 miles) of river, 5,000 km (3,000 miles) of coastline including over two million hectares (five million acres) of coastal water. The Agency has a range of responsibilities and it groups these under three headings:

1. regulatory and environmental management
2. monitoring, assessing, reporting and advising
3. conserving nature and our heritage.

DEFRA – WHAT YOU SHOULD DO

What DEFRA considers today will affect your business tomorrow. You should keep up to date with what they are thinking and doing. DEFRA operates an excellent website where you can find details of the Department's activities, documents and with links to publications and legislation.

✔ Bookmark the DEFRA website. ❏

✔ Visit it regularly and check it for changes that may affect your business. ❏

✔ Note the DEFRA help-line telephone numbers and e-mail address. ❏

Its duties include, for example:

- monitoring the state of pollution and other aspects of the environment
- regulating industrial processes with the greatest pollution potential so as to prevent or minimise pollution to the environment as a whole
- promoting the conservation and enhancement of inland and coastal waters, and their use for recreation
- maintaining or improving non-marine navigation
- administering schemes under producer-responsibility regulations (registration of businesses and exemption schemes, and monitoring and enforcement of associated obligations).

ENVIRONMENT AGENCY HAS A VARIETY OF ROLES [i]

These three examples show the range of functions carried out by the Agency.

Enforcing the law

A County Durham man was fined £5,400 and asked to pay £2,164.44 in costs to the Environment Agency having been found guilty of handling controlled waste on a farm without having a waste management licence.

Durham Magistrates Court heard on 1 June 1999 that the man had been operating an illegal waste transfer station at the farm contrary to sections 33 (1) and (6) of the Environmental Protection Act 1990.

On 17 and 19 January 2000, Environment Agency officers, acting on a tip-off, carried out surveillance using video equipment at the farm. During this time they witnessed loaded skip lorries entering a farm building and reappearing later empty.

Three Agency staff raided the building later on 19 January. Investigations at the site showed that waste was being deposited on the ground before being sorted, bulked and taken to legal landfill sites in the County Durham area. By sorting waste the man stood to gain financially from paying lower landfill disposal costs.

In court, the man pleaded guilty to nine separate charges, receiving a fine of £600 for each offence.

Preventing damage

The Environment Agency has written to all the businesses on the Whitewalls Industrial Estate to remind them of the dangers of pollution to the nearby Colne River and its tributary Swinden Clough.

Agency experts, following up the letters, will visit individual premises. They will advise staff on how to minimise the risks from any potentially polluting activities.

Preventive measures that the Agency will advise on include the management of oil tanks, waste storage and disposal and the proper disposal of trade effluent, as well as underlining the importance of having adequate pollution prevention measures in place.

Tackling floods

A new flood warning system for over 125,000 properties in the centre of Hull was launched in June 2001.

The Environment Agency system is designed to react to a variety of flood scenarios by, for example, sending vital flood warnings to properties at risk of flooding from the River Hull, Barmston Drain and Holderness Drain.

The Agency will use loud-hailer vans, radio and television to warn residents of possible flooding.

The Environment Agency is the leading public organisation for protecting and improving the environment in England and Wales. Its job is to work in a range of ways to achieve this. For example, it regulates industry, maintains flood defences and water resources, and improves wildlife habitats, in addition to many other activities. It also monitors the environment, and makes that information widely available.

The Agency has both a regulatory and an advisory role. As a regulator, it is responsible for enforcing much of the pollution control legislation and the supporting regulations. The Agency implements the IPPC legislation and has considerable powers in this regard including powers of enforcement and prohibition.

THE ENVIRONMENT AGENCY AND SMEs

The Agency operates a special pilot service called 'NetRegs' specifically targeted at

SMEs. The service is web-based and gives practical, sector-specific tips on water, waste and air issues. It aims to clarify the environmental responsibilities of smaller businesses. NetRegs has an easy-to-use graphic interface and it is possible to drill down through the various levels to the legislation itself. You can visit NetRegs at the Agency's website and explore it for yourself: http://www.netregs.environment-agency.gov.uk.

The Agency has a wealth of information available on every aspect of industry's interaction with the environment.

THE ADVISORY COMMITTEE ON BUSINESS AND THE ENVIRONMENT (ACBE)

In May 1991, the Government established the Advisory Committee on Business and the Environment in response to a commitment given in the 1990 Environment White Paper, entitled 'This Common Inheritance'.[ii] The Committee provides for dialogue between Government and business on environmental issues and aims to help mobilise business to adopt good environmental practice and management. The Deputy Prime Minister and the Secretary of State for Trade and Industry jointly appoint the members who serve in a personal capacity.

The Committee has addressed such topics as:

- climate change as a strategic business issue
- carbon trusts and low-carbon technologies
- development of mechanisms to aid in the reduction of greenhouse gases.

THE ROYAL COMMISSION ON ENVIRONMENTAL POLLUTION (RCEP)

This is a highly influential body and has, since it was established by warrant in 1970, played a significant part in shaping the environmental agenda. It exerts its influence through the scientifically authoritative advice that it gives on a range of environmental challenges. It has issued 22 major reports and these have influenced policy and helped to raise public awareness and debate.

As a Royal Commission, RCEP is independent of the government. It advises on matters that sometimes are the UK government's responsibility but in some cases are the responsibility of devolved administrations. It has a close relationship with its parent department, DEFRA, and receives its funding through it.

The Commission sees its role as reviewing and anticipating trends and developments in environmental policies, identifying fields where insufficient attention is being given to problems, and recommending action that should be taken.

The Commission's advice is mainly in the form of reports, which are the outcome of major studies. It also makes short statements on matters it considers of special importance or that arise from studies.

The commission has published 22 reports whose titles include:

- 'Pollution control: progress and problems' (1974)
- 'Air pollution: an integrated approach' (1976)
- 'Nuclear power and the environment' (1976)

- 'Managing waste: the duty of care' (1985)
- 'Emissions from heavy-duty diesel vehicles' (1991)
- 'Incineration of waste' (1993)
- 'Setting environmental standards' (1998)
- 'Energy: the changing climate' (2000).

THE NATURAL ENVIRONMENT RESEARCH COUNCIL (NERC) – RESEARCH OPPORTUNITIES FOR SMEs

The NERC supports and promotes high-quality research in a wide range of environmental sciences. Part of its mission is to advance knowledge and technology and to provide services in sectors such as forestry, hydrocarbons, minerals and fishing. It also provides advice, disseminates knowledge and promotes public understanding of these issues.

The NERC participates in the Small Business Research Initiative (SBRI). The government announced this scheme in July 2000 and it is part of an overall programme to encourage product development and innovation.

From time to time, the NERC announces invitations to tender in the areas within its remit. The scheme gives preference to those who have a proven track record of working in partnership with researchers in universities and research council institutes. It will also favour those with a capability to turn research inputs into new products and services. Contracts are normally capped at £200,000 and are expected to be completed in three years or less.

DEPARTMENT FOR TRADE AND INDUSTRY – INDUSTRY AND THE ENVIRONMENT INTERFACE

The DTI formulates policy relating to industry. It has a number of roles as regards the environment. It promotes awareness of the business potential offered by environmental issues. It also helps businesses plan for the introduction of future international, European and national legislation on the environment. Some of DTI's environmental activities include:

- Fit for the Future campaign – although not strictly concerned with the environment, DTI and the Confederation of British Industry (CBI) are working to increase the number of businesses learning about best practice.
- The Environmental Technology Best Practice Programme (ETBPP) – promotes better environmental performance while working to increase the competitiveness of UK business. It has the goal of stimulating savings for business of around £320 million each year by 2015.
- The Recycling Programme – tackles barriers to increasing the use of recycled materials in manufacturing and strengthens the competitiveness of businesses making use of secondary raw materials.
- The LINK Waste Minimisation Through Recycling, Reuse and Recovery in Industry Programme – is part funded by the DTI with the Engineering Research Council and matching funds from industry.

THE SCOTTISH ENVIRONMENTAL PROTECTION AGENCY (SEPA)

The Scottish Environmental Protection Agency is responsible for environmental protection in Scotland. Established under the

1995 Environmental Protection Act, it became fully operational in 1996. SEPA's main aim is:

'to provide an efficient and integrated environmental protection system for Scotland which will both improve the environment and contribute to the Government's goal of sustainable development.'

SEPA fulfils many of the functions already described for the Environment Agency. It controls pollution, regulates controlled waste movement and disposal and the storage of radioactive materials. SEPA provides advice and guidance aimed at bringing about environmental improvement. It works in partnership with others to achieve its goals.

SEPA issues clear, well-laid out guidance for industry in the form of web-pages, booklets and videos. Topic headings include:

- Regulations and Licensing Information
- Pollution Prevention Guidelines (PPG) Notes
- National Waste Strategy
- Waste Minimisation
- Disposing of PCBs
- Contaminated Land
- Environmental Policies
- Pollution Prevention and Control (Scotland) Regulations
- Hazardous Waste Incineration Directive.

SEPA has a strong regional presence with 20 offices located across the country.

THE ENVIRONMENT AND HERITAGE SERVICE OF NORTHERN IRELAND

This service aims to protect and conserve the natural and built environment and to promote its appreciation for the benefit of present and future generations in Northern Ireland. Its environmental protection activities attempt to safeguard the quality of air, water and land. This involves the enforcement of legislation and additional supporting activities to monitor and report on discharges and emissions. It establishes pollution impacts, sets standards and issues consent licences and authorisations. It has five units dealing with:

1. water quality
2. air quality and noise
3. waste management
4. industrial pollution
5. drinking-water for both public and private supplies.

The most important inspectorate from an SME's perspective is probably the Industrial Pollution and Radiochemical Inspectorate. This has two key regulatory functions:

1. control of pollution and pollution risk from particular industrial processes
2. control of the use, disposal and transport of radioactive substances.

Its main areas of work are:

- industrial pollution control
- Control of Major Accident Hazards (COMAH) regulation
- radioactivity
- environmental monitoring
- radiological emergency
- radon
- legislation.

LOCAL AUTHORITIES

In general, local government is delivered through county and district authorities. England has 34 county councils. There are 32 unitary councils in Scotland. Unitary authorities are all-purpose authorities. There are hundreds of district councils. These bodies have a range of environmental responsibilities. County councils have an overarching role as the developers of strategic plans for their areas. The direction and implementation of these plans has a major environmental impact.

Local authorities play an important role in areas such as:

- waste management including sewerage and drainage
- IPPC application relating to activities listed in Part A2 (a section of the Environment Protection Act listing controlled activities)
- administering the Local Authority Pollution Prevention and Control (LAPPC) system under the Pollution Prevention and Control (England and Wales) Regulations 2000.
- noise and nuisance prevention
- air and water standards
- contaminated land
- transportation through roads, cycle-ways, pathways and parking policies.

Local authorities are responsible for collecting household and commercial waste. They may also play a role in collecting industrial waste if so requested. Increasingly, they are examining ways of reducing waste going to final disposal and are instead searching for more opportunities to recycle materials. The organisation of waste disposal has changed significantly in the late 1990s with the introduction of stricter licensing systems and a shift towards authorities putting waste disposal at arm's length from the central authority.

The local authority uses its powers to make sure that industrial waste-water is pre-treated so that it doesn't damage health, the collection system or the environment. Authorities carry out regular assessments of noise in their areas and they will deal with any noise pollution that they find adversely affects residents and exceeds pre-set limits. The local authorities are also responsible for air pollution other than that dealt with by the Environment Agency. They play a central role in monitoring and reporting on air quality in their areas as well as being responsible for the control of smoke from industrial and commercial premises.

Although planning is outside the scope of this book, local authorities are the primary players in the management of planning in their areas. They have the responsibility of referring developments for environmental assessment where they recognise such a need. They also determine the residential, industrial and agricultural landscape, and through road provision, etc., shape the landscape for businesses in their area.

The local authority will also affect your ability to offer alternative transport options to your workforce. They are involved in the minutiae of transport provision such as the development of cycle-ways.

Access to information

Local authorities must make any information that they hold on the environment in their area available on request. The Environmental Information Regulation of 1992, subsequently amended in 1998, imposes this requirement. They must deal with requests as quickly as possible – within two months at the very most. They may turn down requests for information where it is commercially or personally sensitive or where the documentation is in preparation, confidential or *sub judice*.

Environmental Health Officers

Every district council now has an environmental health officer. Most SMEs are aware of their existence but few will appreciate the broad scope of their functions. EHOs are the enforcement officers for their areas. Larger authorities have a team of EHOs led by a senior or chief EHO.

The EHOs oversee:

- Emissions to the air from businesses not covered by the Environmental Agency. They can limit smoke, dust and grit. They can approve chimney height and they can also declare smoke-control areas.
- The EHOs ensure the quality of drinking water. They check for the presence of pollutants including those of industrial origin as well as biological pathogens.
- EHOs are the officials responsible for the implementation of noise controls in their areas. This includes nuisance caused by noise from construction sites as well as the more mundane loudspeaker, high street pollution.

WHAT YOU NEED TO DO

Most SMEs are unlikely to have day-to-day dealings with government departments. They may deal with the Environment Agency or their local authority. You should:

- Familiarise yourself with your local authority's plans for your area.
- Establish contact with the Environment Agency locally and check out their Netregs website for your sector.
- Know the names and telephone numbers of the key local authority people in your area including the EHOs.
- Watch out for opportunities for development funding from bodies such as the NERC.

CONTACT WEB-SITES WORTH NOTING

Listed below are the website addresses for the main, national organisations. You should also check out your local authority's site.

DEFRA: www.defra.gov.uk

DTI: www.dti.gov.uk

The Environment Agency: www.environment-agency.gov.uk

Environment Agency Netregs: www.netregs.environment-agency.gov.uk

Scottish Environment Agency: www.sepa.org.uk

Northern Ireland Environment and Heritage Service: www.ehsni.gov.uk

The Royal Commission on Environmental Pollution: www.rcep.org.uk

The Natural Environment Research Council: www.nerc.ac.uk

The Advisory Committee on Business and the Environment: (depends on the DEFRA web-site)

NOTES TO CHAPTER 4

i Source: Environment Agency News Releases

ii 'This Common Inheritance', Environment White Paper, Department of the Environment, 1990.

CHAPTER 5

The main legislation *and* what it means for your business – IPC, IPPC, air *and* water

In this chapter, and in the chapter that follows, we examine the main environmental legislation and assess how it affects your business. In this chapter we look at:

- the Integrated Pollution Prevention and Control system (IPPC)
- air pollution and the law
- water pollution.

We'll begin this chapter by examining the IPPC system. This is an important framework system and is in addition to the legislation covering specific types of pollution, i.e., air and water pollution. We give an overview of the general legislation and point out some of the questions you should answer and issues you should note. We steer clear of planning issues and regulations as these form a large body of law in their own right and are outside the scope of this publication. Businesses should note that planning permission might contain environmental conditions.

CONTROLLING POLLUTION – INTEGRATED APPROACHES

The 1990 Environmental Protection Act broke new ground in the legal treatment of pollution in the UK. The Act attempts to deal with the total impact of certain businesses on the environment. It replaces, to a very great extent, the previous piecemeal approach of regulating pollution by the medium, e.g., water, into which it's discharged. The Government has amended the 1990 Act at different times since.

The 1990 Act established the system of Integrated Pollution Control (IPC). This applies to processes that are more likely to cause pollution or that are technologically complex. IPC covers pollution discharges to the air, land and water. The Environment Agency enforces IPC in England and Wales while the Scottish Environment Protection Agency (SEPA) is the responsible body in Scotland. The IPC system is gradually being replaced by the more wide-ranging Integrated Pollution Prevention and Control (IPPC) system based on an EU directive (96/61).

The 1990 Act also introduced a separate regime aimed at controlling air emissions from what are generally less polluting processes. Local authorities enforce this system and it is known as Local Air Pollution Control (LAPC) although it is also known as the Local Authority Air Pollution Control (LAAPC).

The IPC system has two aims:

1. To prevent or minimise pollution by prescribed substances and to neutralise any such substances which are released through the application of Best Available Techniques Not Entailing Excessive Cost (BATNEEC).

2. To ensure that the impact of discharges on the environment as a whole is taken into account.

There are 2,000 prescribed processes covered by the IPC system. The Environmental Protection (Prescribed Processes and Substances) Regulations 1991 contains a schedule of these prescribed processes. The list covers a range of industry sectors from fuel processing through the chemical and heavy metal sectors to agribusiness. This regulation also gives schedules of substances regulated by the Act.

THE IPPC SYSTEM – WHAT WILL CHANGE?

The IPPC system expands the scope of IPC. The UK regime, Pollution Prevention and Control (PPC), will gradually replace the IPC system with the aim of completing the changeover by 2008. The Local Air Pollution Prevention and Control (LAPPC) regime replaces the LAPC and is similar in its approach to IPPC but still focuses on air pollution. PPC incorporates both IPPC and LAPPC.

The new system looks at a broader range of environmental impacts than its IPC predecessor does. It now takes account of: raw material consumption, waste avoidance or minimisation, energy efficiency, accident prevention, the minimisation of noise, heat and vibration, the condition of a plant on closure. The Pollution Prevention and Control Act 1999 gives the Secretary of State the necessary powers to introduce regulations implementing the IPPC. The Pollution Prevention (England and Wales) Regulations 2000 put the Act into effect in England and Wales. Scotland is developing similar regulations.

IPPC applies to installations as opposed to processes. This allows an entire installation to apply for a permit rather than the individual processes within the installation.

More businesses are covered by the IPPC regime. It includes all those currently regulated under IPC, some from LAPC and some new sectors as well. Those added to the process include intensive farming, large pig and poultry units, food and drink manufacturers and a range of waste management facilities. The IPPC applies to installations even where the emissions are trivial.

The Government has divided the responsibility for regulating the IPPC system. The Environmental Agency is responsible for some installations and local authorities retain responsibility for the bulk of installations covered by the LAPC system. The local authorities will continue to regulate air emissions from those not covered by the LAPC regimes. The Scottish Environmental Protection Agency regulates all installations in its territory.

Going BAT

Whilst the IPC applied the Best Available Techniques Not Entailing Excessive Cost (BATNEEC), IPPC uses a slightly different principle known as the Best Available Techniques (BAT). These terms mean:

- **Best** – the most effective techniques for achieving a high level of protection for the environment as a whole;
- **Available** – techniques developed on a scale that allows them to be used in the relevant industrial sector, under economically and technically viable conditions, taking account of the cost and the advantages;

- **Techniques** – include technologies, the installation's design and operation and decommissioning options.

Applying for an IPPC permit

The Government is phasing in the introduction of IPPC. New installations and those undergoing substantial change now need permits. IPC permits continue in force until the IPPC permit is introduced for the installation's sector.

There are a number of steps involved in the process of obtaining an IPPC permit:

- Operators apply to the appropriate regulator – either the Environment Agency or the local authority. The Environment Agency has application forms available on its website.
- A copy of the application is then placed on a public register held in the Environment Agency and the local authority. The public are free to view this.
- Operators must publicise their application through advertisements in one or more local newspapers and in the *London Gazette.*
- Organisations, including those specifically mentioned in the law, and the public can submit comments.
- Following consultation, the regulator either grants a permit, subject to conditions, or rejects the application. Dissatisfied operators can appeal to the Secretary of State.
- A regulator must ensure that operators granted permits adhere to a series of general principles such as the operation of BAT.

Operators should apply for a permit when they have drawn up proper designs. There is nothing to stop an operator beginning construction but they run the risk that the regulatory authority may not accept their approach.

Those applying for a permit must address certain important environmental issues including:

- ensuring proper environmental management
- correct monitoring procedures and practices
- compliance with environmental quality standards and regulations
- efficient energy use and proper waste management
- applying BAT
- accident prevention.

Keeping the permit

Operators have to monitor their performance and show that they are complying with the permit's terms once it is granted. Regulators will also monitor and inspect the installation. They may amend the terms of the permit for various reasons and they may also transfer permits from one operator to another in line with changes in the business's development. They will also review the permit regularly and will act if the plant causes significant pollution.

It's a crime to operate a prescribed plant without a licence. You also have to comply with your permit's conditions once you obtain it and you must inform the regulator if there are any changes to your operation. You contravene these laws at your peril. Conviction in the Magistrates' Court for an offence could result in both:

- a fine of up to £20,000
- a sentence of up to six months.

Conviction in the Crown Court leaves you open to an unlimited fine and imprisonment of up to five years.

Enforcement, suspension and revocation

The regulator will serve an enforcement order on operators when it perceives that they are not meeting or may not meet the conditions of its permit. The order will tell the operator what he or she has to do and will issue a deadline for its completion.

Faced with the threat of serious pollution, the regulator may suspend an operator's permit or activities until satisfied that the danger has been averted properly.

Operators may lose their permits if they don't adhere to the terms that the regulator lays down. Such a revocation may prevent operation but will still leave the operator responsible for any post-operative work necessary.

Responsibilities after closure

Operators must apply to surrender their permits once they cease operation. They must give a site report and identify any changes in the site's condition since the original application. The operator must identify the steps that they have taken to avoid future pollution and/or return the site to an acceptable state.

The regulator may accept a permit's surrender once he is satisfied that an installation is no longer carrying out a prescribed activity and that any potential or real environmental threats have been dealt with. The operator receives a notice and the permit ceases to have effect.

AIR POLLUTION

Our legislators have long recognised the need to control air pollution. Control of air emissions dates back to the Alkali, etc. Works Regulations Act of 1863. This Act concentrated on gross chemical pollution emitted into the air by the early production plants. Since then, successive governments have introduced a number of Clean Air Acts, each building on its predecessors, up to the Clean Air Act of 1993.

The 1990 Environmental Protection Act lists a range of possible circumstances and events that can constitute statutory nuisance relating to air pollution. These include:

- any premises in such a state as to be prejudicial to health or a nuisance
- smoke, fumes or gases emitted from premises so as to be prejudicial to health or a nuisance
- any dust, steam, smell or other effluvia arising on industrial, trade or business premises and being prejudicial to health or a nuisance
- any other matter declared by any enactment to be a statutory nuisance.

The 1995 Environment Act moved the regulation of air pollution to a new level with the requirement that local authorities periodically review air quality in their area and publish the results. This forms part of an overall requirement for a national air quality strategy.

The provisions of the 1993 Clean Air Act control smoke emissions. Part 1 of the Act states:

> 'Dark smoke shall not be emitted from a chimney of any building, and if, on any day, dark smoke is so emitted, the occupier of the building shall be guilty of an offence.'

The Act uses a 'Ringlemann Chart' to define dark smoke. This is a white sheet overprinted with a black grid with various levels of occlusion. The Act defines dark smoke as that smoke that is as dark or darker than shade 2 on the chart.

The dark smoke can come from a chimney, boiler or any part of the premises. The Act recognises important defences for dark smoke emission:

- Smoke caused by lighting up a cold boiler – as long as all possible steps are taken to minimise this.
- Furnace or boiler failure where this is unforeseen and it could not have been prevented before or during the event.
- Unsuitable fuel use due to the unavailability of the correct fuel. The occupier must use the next most suitable fuel and take steps to prevent or minimise dark smoke.

The Clean Air Act requires that all new furnaces are, as far as is practicable, smokeless. It requires that furnaces over a certain size have an arrestment plant to contain grit and dust.

Bonfires obviously create dark smoke and so the 1993 Act controls these activities. In the section dealing with the prohibition of dark smoke from industrial or trade premises, the Act defines such premises as:

> (a) premises used for any industrial or trade purposes; or
> (b) premises not so used on which matter is burnt in connection with any industrial or trade process.

From this it is clear that the Act controls the burning of commercial waste on any premises – not just the premises that generates it.

The Act also addresses chimney height, smoke control zones, motor and other fuels – particularly the sulphur content of oil. It gives local authorities the power to seek information about emissions. The authority can measure and record emissions and engage others to do this on its behalf. The Act specifically prohibits burning insulation from cables to recover the metal contained.

CHECKLIST

✔ Is your operation covered by IPPC? ❏

✔ Are chimneys the correct height and properly tested and maintained? ❏

✔ Are furnaces and boilers maintained and functioning properly? ❏

✔ Are they required to have arrestation for grit or dust? ❏

✔ Are you using the correct fuel and is it burning cleanly? ❏

✔ Do you burn waste? ❏

✔ Are you keeping good records of maintenance and reconditioning of furnaces, etc.? ❏ ❏

✔ Do you have an active smoke, grit and particulate monitoring system in place? ❏

Air pollution and your business

Air emissions are a complex area, legally and to manage. You should look at your business carefully and assess if there are any such emissions escaping and what the constituents are that are involved. If you do produce emissions continuously, regularly or intermittently, then you should use the checklist above.

It is important to pay close attention to air emissions when planning new plant. Obviously new furnaces must be as close to smoke-less as possible. You should make sure that you don't stifle your future development by putting physical barriers to expansion. For example, if you think that you may need a larger furnace or boiler in the future, then make sure that new chimneys are built to accommodate its specification. You should also ensure that you allow adequate space for an arrestment plant if you anticipate that it may be necessary. Check with your local authority and find out what their plans are for smoke control in your area and their likely impact.

WATER LEGISLATION

Water use is a highly regulated activity. It is regulated throughout the water cycle from abstraction to its use for waste disposal. Water is also a finite resource with supplies frequently under pressure – remember the hosepipe bans – and likely to be under increasing pressure in the future.

Water and water-use legislation covers:

- abstraction of water for commercial use
- use of water in industry and the limitation of waste
- disposing of waste-water
- discharges into water bodies
- water conservation standards in manufactured goods such as washing machines.

Common law allows landowners to abstract water from surface water on their land as long as this does not unreasonably damage other peoples' rights relating to that water. You can water cattle without interfering with the rights of those downstream. However, you must return water used in irrigation to the watercourse in the same condition as abstraction. These rights and responsibilities generally refer to smaller water quantities.

The Environment Agency plays a central role in water resource management. It promotes the best use of our water and develops water

BURNING WASTE MAY BREACH LEGISLATION[i]

You can be prosecuted for burning waste under the Environmental Protection Act of 1990 rather than under the Clean Air Act.

Magistrates in Okehampton ordered the owner of a firm producing pallets to pay £750 in fines and costs in a case brought by the Environment Agency.

On 18 December, 2000, the Agency was called to a fire at a premises on an industrial estate. There were wooden pallets burning in a charred skip. The Environment Agency officer instructed an employee at the yard to put out the fire immediately. There was no mains water on site so this took some time as water had to be carried in a small, metal basin.

A few minutes after dousing the fire, the owner of the pallet firm arrived on site but he refused to answer questions from the Agency about the incident.

A few hours later that day, a further complaint was received about another fire at the same location and Environment Agency staff again observed sparks and flames rising from the same skip which had held the previous fire.

The owner of the pallet firm pleaded guilty to burning waste without a licence contrary to Section 33(1)(b)(I) of the Environmental Protection Act 1990. He was fined £400 with £350 costs.

'Despite our previous advice not to burn waste wood at this site, the operator of this business carried on regardless. We will not tolerate this blatant disregard for waste licensing regulations,' said Susan Baird for the Environment Agency.

'Not only was the burning of waste an unlicensed activity that took place close to other businesses and combustible materials but it potentially posed an environmental threat.'

resource management schemes to ensure that it achieves this objective. Apart from developing overall plans, the Agency works at a very specific level dealing with the abstraction and use of water locally.

Commercial water abstraction is generally governed by a licensing system. At present, the government is reviewing the current controls on water abstraction with a view to rationalising and improving the process. In general, you cannot abstract significant amounts of water from a freshwater source without applying for a licence, advertising this widely and then meeting the Environment Agency's requirements. The Agency itself will take other water users' needs into account. It will consider representations received on foot of the advertising together with any other relevant information.

The Water Resources Act 1991 has as one of its objectives maintaining and improving the quality of controlled waters (section 83). The Environment Agency plays a key role in achieving this objective. The Act covers virtually all water in England and Wales including freshwater, groundwater, coastal waters and territorial waters.

The Act forbids anyone from causing or knowingly permitting any poisonous, noxious or polluting matter or any solid waste matter to enter any controlled waters. The different subsections of the Act further prescribe the disposal of trade or sewage effluent onto land or into any waters of a lake or pond which are not inland freshwaters. It is also possible to contravene the Act by impeding water flow such that it results in pollution due to other causes or other consequential pollution.

The Environment Agency may issue prohibition notices preventing a discharge or setting conditions on that discharge. It is also an offence if the effluent or matter discharged:

- contains a prescribed substance or a prescribed concentration of such a substance; or
- derives from a prescribed process or from a process involving the use of prescribed substances or the use of such substances in quantities which exceed the prescribed amounts.

You can discharge pollution into water under certain circumstances such as an emergency where this is necessary to save life or protect health. Taking all reasonable, practical steps to avert the discharge and furnishing details to the Agency as soon as possible afterwards will also be taken into account when the Agency decides whether or not to seek a prosecution.

You are not allowed to uproot, cut or destroy vegetation in any waterway. Nor can you remove any of the bottom, channel, bed or deposit from a waterway.

Sewers and drains

Discharges into the drainage and sewerage system are of great importance to SMEs. The 1991 Water Industry Act forbids you putting anything into the sewerage system that may damage it in any way. You cannot use the sewerage system to dispose of chemicals, waste fuels, hot water or other hot or inflammable liquids.

Chapter III of the Water Industry Act 1991 addresses the issue of trade effluents in great detail. You need consent to discharge effluent into the system. Operators have to apply for this consent and the sewerage service provider may impose conditions on an operator. Certain effluents are categorised as 'special' and the service provider must refer any applications

OIL SPILL POSES A THREAT TO GROUNDWATER[ii]

Groundwater forms part of the water resource. It is possible to pollute water by polluting the land over groundwater.

On 16 May 2001, magistrates in Dorset ordered a West Midlands-based distribution firm to pay £2,041 in fines and costs after a diesel spill in Dorset.

Earlier, on 30 October 2000, the Environment Agency had been alerted to a fuel spill at a premises near Bournemouth. A fuel storage tank was found to be leaking diesel.

Around 200 litres of diesel had escaped after a pallet, stacked near the storage tank, had toppled from its pile in high wind and broken a gauge on the tank causing the fuel to leak out and onto the ground.

It was the second time in six weeks that oil had spilled from the same tank. Environment Agency officers advised the firm to make improvements to its fuel storage facilities and to clean up the land that had become contaminated with fuel.

Magistrates heard the West Midlands company plead guilty to causing polluting matter to enter groundwater contrary to Section 85 (1) and (6) of the Water Resources Act 1991. The company was fined £1,000 and ordered to pay £1,041 costs.

'It is essential that fuel storage tanks are properly looked after and the risk of pollution is kept to a minimum,' said Dave Womack for the Environment Agency.

'This sort of incident is easily preventable and if any firms are concerned about their fuel storage facilities, they can contact the Agency for advice on how to minimise the risk of needless pollution such as this.'

involving these substances to the Environment Agency.

Operators have to provide the sewerage undertaker with information on the sewage system in their plant and how they intend to use it.

Sewerage undertakers must maintain a register of consents, agreements and notices and this must be available, at all reasonable times, for inspection by the public free of charge at the offices of the undertaker.

SEEPAGE HAS CHILLING EFFECTS[iii]

This case demonstrates how important it is to check for leaks, spills and incorrect disposal of liquid waste.

Magistrates fined a food company £5,000 after the company admitted polluting a stream, near Preston, with rusty water from a chiller unit (30 May 2001).

The Leeds-based company was also ordered to pay £639 costs to the Environment Agency, which brought the prosecution.

Julie Goulbourne, prosecuting for the Environment Agency, told the Magistrates' Court in Leyland how a member of the public reported orange discoloration of the stream on 12 March 2000.

An Agency Environment Protection Officer (EPO) attended the scene, and found the stream was severely discoloured with what appeared to be rusty deposits.

The court heard how a number of surface water drains, designed to carry only clean rainwater, drained into this particular brook near the polluted area. One was from the company being prosecuted.

On the company's premises, the EPO found evidence of rusty stains over a significant area next to a chiller unit and a surface water drain. A representative of the company told the EPO that the drain went to the foul sewer system, and not to the river, but subsequent tests using coloured dyes proved the drain led to the brook.

Later that month, on 29 March, the company wrote to the Environment Agency to explain how repairs to the chiller unit made it necessary to empty the chilled-water tank. The company said it knew there would be a spillage of waste-water during the repairs, but that it believed the drain ran to the foul sewer, and not the river.

The court was told that about 400m of the stream was affected by the pollution, with the stream bed contaminated with iron.

Preventing water pollution

Preventing pollution is an important aim of most environmental legislation. The Water Resources Act 1991 gives powers to the Secretary of State to prohibit a person from having or controlling polluting substances and, where they have these substances already, they may be required to carry out work to ensure that they are appropriately dealt with.

The Secretary of State, following consultation with the appropriate bodies, may declare a water protection zone. This allows the Environmental Agency to regulate activities in the area: to investigate, prevent or restrict specific activities as it sees necessary for the protection of the area.

The Environment Agency also protects waterways through the IPPC process. The relevant Acts define prescribed substances and the level that is allowed in a water body. These range from heavy metals through to organic chemicals and pesticides. The Agency can also prosecute polluters under the Salmon and Freshwater Act 1975 within which it is an offence to release 'any liquid or solid matter (into the waterway) to such an extent as to cause the waters to be poisonous or injurious to fish or the spawning grounds, spawn or food of fish.'

Nitrate sensitive areas

The Water Resources Act 1991 makes specific mention of nitrate pollution. The Act allows the appropriate Minister to declare a nitrate-sensitive area. As the name implies, this section of the Act aims to protect waterways from nitrate pollution. This mainly affects farmers and foresters, and the Act allows the designated Minister to enter into agreements with land users to achieve this objective.

Some things you should check

Water is everywhere and so most businesses run some risk of polluting it. You should check that you have the appropriate authorisation to take whatever water you use and that you are disposing of it safely. You should also make sure that:

- you know the layout of your drains and sewers
- waste chemicals are separated from the waste water system and properly disposed of
- that any yard run-off going into storm drains is free from pollution
- storage tanks and other containers are at a distance and downhill from waterways
- you collect waste oil from trucks and other machinery and dispose of it safely.

NOTES TO CHAPTER 5

i Source: Environment Agency news release, "Firm owner fined for burning waste", Ben Woodhouse, June 2001.

ii Source: Environment Agency news release, "Midlands firm fined after fuel storage tank leak", Bridget Norris, May 2001.

iii Source: Environment Agency news release, "Court fines food company £5,000 for Lancashire stream pollution", Steve Broughton, May 2001.

Further regulation – waste, noise, contaminated land *and* tax

This chapter takes a look at some more of the legislation affecting SMEs. We also look at some budgetary mechanisms aimed at promoting changes in behaviour. The areas examined are:

- waste and recycling packaging
- noise and alarms
- issues surrounding contaminated land
- taxation and the environment.

WASTE AND RECYCLING

Virtually all processes generate some form of waste. Disposing of waste will become increasingly difficult as EU directives and UK legislation attempt to reduce waste and encourage recycling. In this section, we consider the regulations that control trade and industrial waste disposal. The broader issues of the operation and management of waste disposal facilities such as incinerators or landfill sites are beyond the scope of this publication.

Landfill is the cheapest and most common means used for industrial and commercial waste disposal. It is used for most wastes with the exception of corrosive materials, liquids, flammable, explosive or unstable materials, clinical waste or tyres. However, the 1999 EU Directive on the use of landfill will greatly reduce the quantity and type of waste that will be disposed of in landfill in the future. The Directive aims to achieve a 75 per cent reduction in biodegradable municipal waste by 2020 (using the 1995 figure as the baseline).

Currently, local authorities and others levy a landfill tax based on tonnage. This is £2 per tonne for inert waste and £11 per tonne for active waste. This tax will increase annually by £1 per tonne until 2004.

Current legislation recognises several categories of waste including household, commercial, industrial, special, directive, hazardous and difficult waste. It is often difficult to establish the precise make-up of any waste – particularly industrial waste. Businesses are well advised to examine what waste they produce currently and satisfy themselves that they know what constitutes the waste that they produce. You should pay particular attention to any hazardous or potential dangerous materials or mixtures.

The 1990 Environmental Protection Act is the starting point for most modern UK legislation regulating waste disposal on land. Its broad aims are best summarised in section 33 entitled 'Prohibition on unauthorised or harmful depositing, treating or disposal, etc. of waste' where it states that a person shall not:

(a) deposit controlled waste, or knowingly cause or knowingly permit controlled waste to be deposited in or on any land, unless a waste management licence is in force and the deposit is in accordance with the licence

(b) treat, keep or dispose of controlled waste, or knowingly cause or knowingly permit controlled waste to be treated, kept or disposed of
   (i)   in or on any land, or
   (ii)   by means of any mobile plant
   except under and in accordance with a waste management licence

(c) treat, keep or dispose of controlled waste in a manner likely to cause pollution of the environment or harm human health.

Controlled waste

Controlled waste means waste from house-holds, commerce or industry, although house-holders are exempt from the duty of care for their own household waste.

Duty of care

All businesses producing, moving or disposing of waste have a duty of care under the 1990 Environmental Protection Act. This duty of care applies even after you pass the waste on to someone else in the chain. You must ensure that they comply with the regulations and that they dispose of it in a safe, legal way.

Businesses must prepare a written description of the waste that they produce and this should travel with the waste. This must cover the type of waste, how it is contained, transfer times, etc.

Dealing with waste

The Code of Practice (Waste Management Duty of Care)[i] lists the following questions as a way of checking if there is a waste problem:

- Does the waste need a special container to prevent its escape or to protect it from the elements?
- What type of container suits it and what material can the container be made of?
- Can it safely be mixed with any other waste or are there wastes with which it should not be mixed?
- Can it safely be crushed and transferred from one vehicle to another?
- Can it safely be incinerated or are there special requirements for its incineration such as minimum temperature and combustion time?
- Can it be disposed of safely in a landfill site with other waste?
- Is it likely to change its physical state during storage or transport?

FAST FOOD SHOP OWNER'S PROSECUTION SHOWS THAT YOU MUST KEEP TRACK OF YOUR WASTE[ii]

Disposing of trade and business waste can be a burden. Be careful when you ask someone to take that burden from you. You still have responsibilities under law that travel with the rubbish.

On 23 May 2001, Leeds Magistrates' Court fined two shopkeepers for a waste-related offence. The court heard that the owners of a fast food restaurant did not make sure that the waste from their premises was being taken away by an authorised person.

They also admitted failing to ensure that a transfer note was completed for the transfer of waste. All the charges contravened section 34 of the 1990 Environmental Protection Act.

They were each fined £400 and ordered to pay £800 costs.

The court heard that a customer visited the premises and offered to remove the restaurant waste daily. The customer gave an invoice for the cost of the waste removal each month. However, it did not contain the information required by the law.

The Environment Agency's investigation began when there were complaints that waste, packaging and cooking oil drums had been found in a car park nearby.

There was no evidence that the defendants had been personally responsible for the waste finding its way to the car park, but the shopkeepers had failed under Duty of Care to make sure their waste was being disposed of by an authorised person.

PACKAGING – REDUCTION, RECYCLING AND RECOVERY

Government and the EU have recognised the damage caused to the environment by excessive packaging on products and materials. A 1994 EU Directive[iii] set targets for the reduction in packaging in member states. The Directive wants national governments to recover over half of packaging waste and to recycle between a quarter and a half of this waste. Recovery includes recycling, energy recovery and composting (biodegradable materials).

The EU Directive has been put into effect through the Producer Responsibility Obligations (Packaging Waste) Regulations 1997. Further amendments have added to this regulation since then.

YOU CAN'T SKIP YOUR WASTE RESPONSIBILITIES

You can still be responsible for waste after it passes from your premises as the following case shows. Companies should pay special attention to ensuring that the body receiving waste knows what it contains.

On 23 May 2001, Leeds Magistrates' Court fined a timber company £2,000 and ordered it to pay a further £3,216 in costs.

The company admitted a charge under the Environmental Protection Act following spillage from a skip containing the company's waste.

The court heard that a skip driver for Leeds City Council collected a skip from the firm's premises and took it to the council's bulk transfer station site on Kirkstall Road. As he tipped out the skip, a large number of drums fell out and there was a spillage of liquid and a strong solvent-like smell.

The site manager segregated off the area and called the Environment Agency. A total of twenty-two 25-litre drums, two 20-litre drums and eight five-litre drums were found still to have contents. Agency officers took samples and some of them revealed organic solvents, which were classified as special waste.

The court was told that the Kirkstall Road site was not licensed to take special waste. The company admitted that as the producer of controlled waste, including special waste, it had failed to take all reasonable measures in the circumstances to prevent any contravention by any other person of section 33 of the Environmental Protection Act 1990, namely informing the waste carrier of the presence of special waste.

Who is affected by the packaging regulation?

This regulation affects everyone in the packaging chain from manufacturers of packaging materials, box makers and others who convert materials into packaging, packers and fillers, retailers and importers. Those with an annual turnover below £2 million or those handling less than 50 tonnes of packaging or packaging materials annually are exempt from this regulation.

PACKAGING REGULATIONS BEING ENFORCED[IV]

This case shows that the Environment Agency is actively pursuing those companies that fail to register properly.

Bath Magistrates' Court ordered a local printing company to pay £880 costs and served it with a two-year conditional discharge for failing to meet its obligation to cut down on waste. The case was heard on the 5 May 2001.

Legislation brought in by the Government in 1997 stipulates that firms with an annual turnover of £2 million that handle over 50 tonnes of packaging a year must contribute to reducing the amount of waste packaging sent to landfill. Businesses meeting this criteria must register annually either with the Environment Agency or an approved scheme.

An Agency investigation found that the company failed to register on time last year and failed to comply with packaging recovery obligations for the year before.

At Bath Magistrates' Court, the company pleaded guilty to failing to register with the Environment Agency or an approved scheme as required under regulations 3(5)(a) and 5 of the Producer Responsibility Obligations (Packaging Waste) Regulations 1997. The company was served a two-year conditional discharge and was ordered to pay £880 costs.

What are you required to do?

Packaging must be minimal subject to safety, hygiene and the need to pack the product appropriately for its use and for the consumer. There must be a minimum of noxious materials and heavy metals contained in the packaging. It must be recoverable by at least one of: material recycling, incineration with energy recovery, composting, or biodegradation.

You can comply with the law in two ways:

1. you may register directly with the appropriate agency, the Environment Agency, SEPA or the Environment and Heritage Service, or

2. you can join a compliance scheme to carry out your responsibilities on your behalf.

Registering directly

To register directly you must:

1. Register with the appropriate agency, provide data on packaging handled in the previous year and pay a fee (currently £950).

59

2. Recover a specified amount of post-consumer packaging waste and recycle a specified amount of material-specific waste.

3. Receive certificates for these tonnages.

4. Submit details of these tonnages to the registration agency in its certificate of compliance.

Using a compliance scheme

Compliance schemes may provide companies with an easier way of dealing with packaging waste. They can save you time and money by taking over your obligations and managing them on your behalf. Compliance schemes will:

- take over your business's legal responsibilities
- register your company with the appropriate environmental agency
- pay your agency fee
- verify the data that you supply
- agree contracts with reprocessors
- demonstrate your business's compliance
- provide your business with a compliance certificate.

Electrical and electronic equipment

Waste regulation is becoming more sector- and industry-specific. One important piece of legislation deals with waste electrical and electronic equipment. This legislation will give effect to an EU directive known as the WEEE (Waste Electrical and Electronic Equipment) Directive. This directive coupled with a sister one limiting the levels of hazardous substances in electrical and electronic equipment will have significant impact on the industry.

The WEEE directive applies to:

- large household appliances including refrigerators and washing machines
- small household appliances such as vacuum cleaners, toasters, clocks, etc.
- information technology and telecommunications equipment
- consumer equipment such as TVs, video recorders, Hi-fi systems
- lighting equipment
- electrical and electronic tools with the exception of large-scale stationary industrial tools
- toys, leisure and sports equipment
- medical devices excluding all implanted and infected products
- monitoring and control instruments
- automatic dispensers.

The directive envisages that distributors will have to take back an equivalent product, free of charge, when they deliver a new product. The collection systems will have to be in place 30 months after the directive comes into effect. There are set recycling targets for the various products. For example, 80 per cent of category 1 products will have to be recovered with a reuse/recycle rate of 75 per cent.

NOISE

Commerce is generally a noisy business. From the 'beeb, beeb, beeb' of reversing lorries to the lonely wail of a burglar alarm, there are many sounds that can annoy neighbours and workers alike. Noise is often treated as a nuisance and people can seek redress through the courts. Local Authorities may also use bye-laws to regulate noise, ranging from barking dogs to garden equipment, in their areas. The Control of Pollution Act (COPA) 1974 addressed the issue of noise pollution. Part III focuses on noise. The Act addresses:

- the control of noise on construction sites
- designation of noise abatement zones and measurement of noise levels
- noise from plant and machinery.

The Act covers all construction activities including maintenance, demolition and dredging work. It allows the local authority to serve a notice imposing requirements as to the way in which the works are to be carried out. Those carrying out the work may apply for prior consent and thus, if it is granted, protect themselves.

Retail businesses need to pay special attention to the regulations regarding noise in the street. It prohibits using a loudspeaker in a street:

- between the hours of nine in the evening and eight in the following morning for any purpose;
- at any other time, for the purpose of advertising any entertainment, trade or other business.

The term street is broadly defined and means a highway and any other road, footway, square or court which is for the time being open to the public. There are a number of exceptions to this general prohibition including the emergency services or as a warning device. It also allows travelling showmen to use loudspeakers on land which is being used for the purposes of a pleasure fair.

Local authorities must inspect their areas from time to time to assess whether or not there is noise pollution or nuisance and they must also investigate any complaints about noise. If they are satisfied that a nuisance exists then they must serve a notice on the person responsible.

Local authorities may also create Noise Abatement Zones (NAZs). These protect the quality of life in an area and prevent a worsening of the noise environment. NAZs are not widely used and are likely to be changed in future legislation.

Plant, machinery and noise from premises

The COPA gives wide powers to the Secretary of State to regulate noise from plant and machinery. This allows orders for the use of noise reduction devices and arrangements and the application of standards, specifications, etc., for plant and machinery.

The later, 1990 Environmental Protection Act states that noise emitted from a premises may constitute a statutory nuisance. Operators should note that what applies to noise can also refer to vibrations. Local authorities may take both preventative and remedial action. People may also take action independently under common law.

Planning and noise

Planning authorities may include conditions governing noise levels when granting planning permissions. Planning authorities consult widely and will take submissions on noise pollution into account in their deliberations.

Alarms and false alarms

Businesses receive justifiable criticism in relation to the disturbance caused by intruder and other alarms – particularly where the alarms are false. The Control of Noise (Code of Practice on Noise from Audible Intruder Alarms) Order 1981[viii] addresses this issue. What you should do is:

- appoint two key holders, other than the owner, who know how to turn off the system
- inform the local police of their names, addresses and telephone numbers
- notify the police of changes of contact details within 24 hours
- make sure that key holders are able to respond in 20 minutes or as agreed with the local authority
- inform the local authority that there is an alarm on the premises and the name of the police station where the details are kept.

If you fail to respond in the required time, or if you have frequent false alarms, then the local authority may issue an abatement order to fit an automatic cut-out system on the alarm. The police may also penalise you if your alarm is connected directly to the police station and it generates a number of false alarms. The number allowed before action varies from area to area.

The alarm owner must ensure that the system is installed and maintained in accordance with the proper British Standard.

CONTAMINATED LAND

Contaminated land is an important environmental issue and of concern to any business owning or occupying land that is used or has been used for commercial purposes. As the phrase implies, contaminated land describes any land containing harmful substances in sufficient concentration to pose a risk to humans, animals or the environment generally. The contamination may be chemical, biological (e.g., pathogens that pose a health risk) or physical (e.g., asbestos dust, gases or flammable materials such as resins or wood dust). Frequently, contaminated land may combine some or all of these risks to create a more complex environmental problem.

Contamination can happen for a range of reasons for example:

- leaks or spillages
- waste disposal
- emission (e.g., stack emissions)
- contaminated groundwater entering a site
- other's pipe or waste contaminating a site
- imported soil or waste used for in-fill, capping, etc.

Contaminated land can threaten the environment in a number of ways. For example, wind and rain can spread materials around the immediate neighbourhood and even further afield. Percolation into groundwater poses a threat to whole waterways. Animals can ingest or absorb materials and concentrate them in the food chain. People can come in contact with the hazard directly by walking on or handling the ground.

The Government is encouraging the redevelopment of brownfield sites. These sites are generally closer to cities and towns and are ideal for commercial and residential use. The policy intention is to reduce urban sprawl and alleviate the need for people to travel long distances to reach their work or amenities by providing housing in towns and cities.

Legislation dealing with contaminated land

The current legislation dealing with contaminated land is contained in Environmental Protection Act 1995. This adds new sections to the previous Environmental Protection Act 1990 and is often referred to as Part IIA.

The legislation requires local authorities to inspect their area from time to time, identify contaminated land and, where necessary, designate it as a special site. Special sites are those most severely contaminated or facing the most difficult remediation problems. They include sites causing pollution to controlled waters, those where explosives have been manufactured or processed, and those contaminated with waste acid tar. The Environment Agency or the SEPA are the enforcing authority for special sites.

The law requires that local authorities identify the risk involved. The presence of a contaminant isn't sufficient in itself. There must be a receptor (e.g., a person or animal) and a pathway whereby the pollutant can reach the receptor. These two together constitute a pollutant linkage.

The legislation does not require that contaminated land is returned to a virginal state. It takes a more pragmatic approach in that the land should be restored to a level appropriate to its future use. Obviously, where there is serious pollution, the local authority can insist on immediate action.

Where the local authority identifies a contaminated site it will then serve notice to the agencies, the appropriate persons, owners and occupiers. There then follows a consultation process of at least three months. The authority will ultimately serve a remediation notice if no voluntary agreement is reached.

Who pays for remediation?

The local authority will investigate and identify the owners and occupiers of contaminated land. They will also explore the history of the site and try to establish who actually caused or knowingly permitted the contamination: these are known as Class A appropriate persons. Class A people will normally be liable for remediation costs on the basis of the polluter pays principle (PPP). However, it may not be possible to identify the original polluter. For example, some land may have been contaminated several centuries ago. If the local authority cannot identify the Class A person or persons, then responsibility for remediation falls on the current owner or occupier, known as the Class B appropriate person.

The legislation aims to ensure that costs are apportioned fairly. There may be several Class A appropriate persons responsible for polluting a site. The local authority will try to establish costs in a way that reflects the pollution caused by the different individuals.

In some cases, the local authority or the Environment Agency may carry out the remediation itself. In these circumstances, it will pursue the appropriate persons for the costs involved.

What should you do

You should carry out a thorough check on land you plan to buy for development:

1. In the first instance, you should research the history of the site and see if there are indications that it may have been polluted in any way in the past.
2. You should establish who owned it and what businesses they operated. This information may help to identify Class A appropriate persons.
3. Try to establish the type and extent of contamination through sample analysis and expert opinion.

4. Assess the degree of remediation needed to bring the land back to a state suitable for the development proposed.

5. Determine how best the land may be remediated. Environmental consultants offer advice on the best ways to carry out this task.

The main ways of remediating a site are:

- removal – where you excavate the contaminated soil and replace it with clean material
- dilution – where you reduce the toxic levels by adding clean filler and thus reducing the concentration of pollutant
- isolating the contaminants and thus breaking the pollutant linkage
- treating – there are a range of treatments available to remediate land. These include biotechnological and chemical technologies.

TAXES AND INCENTIVES – THE ALTERNATIVE LEGISLATIVE APPROACH

We don't normally think of the budget as a piece of environmental legislation. More and more the Government, specifically the Chancellor, is using the tax system as an instrument for environment regulation and management.

The 2001 Budget showed how the Government can use tax and other incentives to change the way that people and businesses behave. One of the key elements in this regard is the introduction of a climate change levy. This levy aims to encourage the non-domestic sector to become more energy-efficient and so reduce carbon emissions. The levy package aims to save at least five million tonnes of carbon a year by 2010.

Climate change levy and energy saving

The climate change levy applies to non-domestic use of energy. All revenues collected are recycled to business through a 0.3 per cent cut in employers' national insurance contributions and additional support for energy-saving technologies. The products subject to the levy are electricity, gas, liquified petroleum gas (LPG) and solid fuels.

The 2001 Budget provides direct help to businesses aiming to reduce energy consumption. It gives 100 per cent first year capital allowances for investments in designated energy-saving technologies. Eight technology categories are eligible: motors, refrigeration, lighting, boilers and add-ons, variable speed drives, thermal screens, pipe insulation, and good quality combined heat and power. The Budget promises to update this list annually and add further technologies if they prove to offer cost-effective improvements and satisfactory methods of certification.

The Government is changing the VAT regime to encourage a more environmentally friendly approach. The 2000 Budget reduced VAT from 17.5 per cent to 5 per cent on the installation of specific energy-saving materials such as insulation, draught stripping, hot water and central heating system controls and solar panels. It also introduced a 5 per cent reduced rate of VAT for the grant-funded installation of new central heating systems and their maintenance and repair, and heating appliances in the homes of the less well-off.

Supporting new technologies

The alternative energy business received a major boost in the 2001 Budget. The

Government aims to have 10 per cent of the UK's electricity supplied from renewable sources by 2010. This is an approximately four-fold increase on the 1999 figure. The 2001 Budget made a number of changes that help the renewable energy sector. These include:

- an exemption from the climate change levy
- £100-million fund to promote environmental technologies including support for renewables such as off-shore wind, energy crops and solar power
- a requirement that electricity suppliers secure a specified proportion of electricity from renewable generators.

Addressing travel and transport

Annually, we clock up 375 billion car-miles in the UK. Business-use accounts for 16 per cent of this figure. The cars chosen by companies for employees also affect private car purchase, both through the second-hand market and the power that fleet purchasing exerts on manufacturers.

The Government is reforming company car taxation with the income tax charge on a company car being based on a percentage of the car's list price graduated according to the level of the car's carbon dioxide emissions. The charge builds, from 15 per cent to a maximum of 35 per cent, in 1 per cent steps for every 5 gram/km of carbon dioxide. The new tax regime also addresses diesel cars, mileage allowance and other motoring costs. The changes favour more environmentally friendly motoring.

Green travel is a relatively new concept in business. Government is promoting it through the tax system. It has increased the National Insurance contribution-free mileage rate that employers can pay for using a cycle on business trips. It is also encouraging car-sharing on business trips with a new passenger rate of two pence per mile. It is lowering the threshold for works buses qualifying for tax exemptions from 12 to nine passenger seats to help encourage employers in smaller companies set up travel plans allowing their employees to travel to work without using cars. Government has also adjusted the VAT rates to increase the range of alternative transport options to work.

What does this mean for SMEs?

Tax changes and financial incentives are the clearest communication a Government gives of its intentions. Budgets are no longer the stand-alone programmes of previous decades. They are now part of a rolling programme that builds on previous initiatives. This approach means that we can read the Government's plans clearly in its current Budget strategy. This presents SMEs with a number of opportunities. Some questions worth answering are:

- Could my company benefit from the first-year capital allowances for the designated energy-saving technologies?
- Should we be sourcing alternative energy sources to avoid the potential future impact of the climate change levy?
- Is there a business opportunity for my company in renewable energy?
- If your business is involved in energy products, should you start promoting lower VAT-rated products more aggressively?
- Does your company need to review its car fleet policy to reduce costs and maximise savings under the new regime? Employees won't thank you if they end up with a greater tax bill in the future.
- Is it time to get a company bus and/or develop travel planning, car pooling, etc., for employees?

- Should you cycle to some of your business meetings?

NOTES TO CHAPTER 6

i   *'Waste Management, The Duty of Care. A Code of Practice',* London, The Stationery Office, 1996.

ii Source: Environment Agency news release, Fast Food Shopkeepers fined, Sue Norton, May 2001.

iii Source: Environment Agency news release, Timber firm fined for waste offence, Sue Norton, May 2001.

iv Source: Environment Agency news release, Bath firm pleads guilty to breaching recycling regulations, Ben Woodhouse, June 2001.

Practical first steps

This chapter aims to help you to assess what impact your business has on the environment at present, and what the possible impacts of environmental regulations on your business are. It sets out the steps you should take to ensure compliance with current and future regulations. It helps you answer the following questions:

- How do I find out how I'm doing at present?
- What are the strategic and business issues that I face?
- How do I assess the environmental impact of my business operations?
- How do I put a proper environmental monitoring system in place?

ENVIRONMENTAL REGULATION ISN'T IMPORTANT TO MY BUSINESS

Environmental legislation affects every business in some way. Yet there are plenty of companies, particularly SMEs, who are unaware of their legal responsibilities and have still to take steps to ensure that they comply with the law. If this sounds like your company, then you are risking prosecution, wasting resources, and possibly putting future business at risk.

A quick scan of the previous chapters should show you where environmental legislation may impact upon your business. In this chapter we take a closer look at how you might decide whether or not key legislation affects you. Remember, ignorance is not an excuse in law and if you are in doubt about your responsibilities you should investigate them further immediately.

WHERE DO I START?

You should start by looking at your industry sector and your place in it. Some sectors are more rigorously controlled than others are. Your business may come under the IPPC system. This covers most of those regulated by the Environment Agency under IPC together with those coming under the Local Air Pollution Control (LAPC). In addition, those governed by the waste-management licensing regime also come under the IPPC system. If your process already comes under IPC, then you will be converting to IPPC by 2007. There is a timetable for this changeover with deadlines for each activity. Refer back to Chapter 5 to find out more about applying for an IPPC permit.

IPPC covers a wide range of activities including:

- activities involving asbestos, carbon, carbon disulphide or ammonia
- chemical (organic, inorganic, pharmaceutical and fertiliser) production
- cement and lime production
- ceramics
- coating activities, printing and textile treatment
- combustion
- explosives manufacture
- ferrous and non-ferrous metals manufacture
- gasification, liquefaction and refining activities
- glass and glass-fibre activities
- intensive farming
- mineral fibre activities
- paper, pulp and board production
- plant-health products and biocides
- surface treatment of metals and plastic materials
- tar and bitumen manufacture
- timber activities
- treatment of animal and vegetable matter and food industries
- waste disposal and recovery and the production of fuel from waste.

The processes coming under IPC include:

- chemical industry
- fuel production processes, combustion processes including power generation
- metals production and processing
- mineral industry
- waste disposal and recycling
- other industry processes including those relating to the application of phenyl-based coatings on ships and boats, di-isocyanate manufacture and toluene di-isocyanate use in polyurethane flame bonding, paper production and related processes, processing animal hides and skins, tar and bitumen, timber preservation.

TAKE AN OVERVIEW OF YOUR BUSINESS

Strategic implications

Begin with your overall business strategy. You should examine the strategic implications of current or potential regulations on your business. For example, if you produce household electrical goods or manufacture goods using CFCs or PCBs, then you must be aware of and work within the specific regulations affecting these products or substances. You should also track forthcoming regulations and assess their likely impact. Most new regulations are phased in over a period and you need to adapt your strategy to accommodate these changes. You may have to plan for the upgrading or replacement of equipment to meet new standards or you may have to restructure your production process. Such changes can be expensive, particularly if you don't integrate them into your overall business plan.

Meeting the relevant regulations is the minimum: you should also consider how environmental issues may have strategic implications for your business. Most of our businesses are part of an overall industry business chain. Your business customers may plan to introduce environmental regulations of their own. You need to ensure that you can meet such regulations. Buyers are not necessarily aware of planned policy changes and you should talk with the technical and environmental personnel working for your key business customers.

If you retail direct to consumers, you should examine emerging trends. Environmentally friendly products may attract more customers. If competitors offer an environmentally friendly option, will you be able to compete and what impact will it have on your margins? At present, environmentally friendly products generally have better margins. You should note that as such products become the norm, so the benefit will decline. Early entrants gain the maximum benefit.

Business overview

If you manufacture or produce some product, it must conform to the regulations that apply to it. A key step is to ensure that your product fully meets performance, labelling, component and other regulations. Regulations concerning energy performance are becoming stricter and you must ensure that you meet these fully.

You need to look at every aspect of your

POINT TO NOTE

Remember that if you export products, they must meet the regulations that apply in your destination country. In addition, they may have to conform to the environmental regulations that apply in countries through which the product passes. This may affect your transportation and shipping choices.

---

business to understand what impacts it has on the environment and where these occur. The best place to start is your internal business chain of inputs, processes and outputs. You must explore how your business affects its immediate environment. You must also consider what happens to your products when they leave your company. In certain circumstances, you must also consider what will happen when your company ceases operation. For example, will you face land remediation problems once you leave your site?

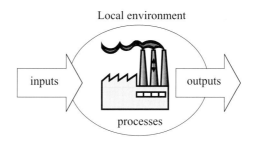

GETTING ON WITH YOUR NEIGHBOURS

Nuisance is the main cause of problems with neighbours. Nuisance includes noise, smells, smoke, dust, and light pollution. As mentioned earlier, nuisance can even arise from pigeons using your premises for roosting! Businesses, particularly small businesses, sometimes encounter difficulties when they move premises and recommence activities. A business may find that what was acceptable in its former premises now constitutes a nuisance in the new location.

You should begin at the perimeter of your premises and try to see where there is potential for nuisance to occur. Do this a number of times as activities, fumes and noise levels vary at different times both daily and seasonally. Sometimes, for example in warm weather, staff may leave entrances, skylights or windows open and thus cause intermittent nuisance to your neighbours.

It's a good idea to get someone from outside the business to give a view of your operations. They may spot obvious potential or actual nuisance that you have become used to and just don't see. We often become acclimatised to the fumes and noise of our own business. Someone from another business profession will spot these immediately.

Where you find nuisance, make sure that you take steps to reduce or eliminate it straight away. The law generally expects that these will be proportional to the degree of nuisance and should not entail undue costs.

Cut down on noise

Companies based in business parks or industrial estates generally have less nuisance problems than those in mixed developments or in city, town or village centres. Noise can be a major source of irritation, particularly in built-up areas. Here are some simple things that will help reduce noise in any area:

- Keep delivery bays, external doors, windows and skylights closed.
- Shut internal doors to reduce noise spreading to adjoining premises.
- Use damping screens where necessary.
- Put your noisiest activities at the centre of the building or in a location where they are unlikely to cause disturbance.
- Workers like to listen to radios while they work – make sure that these are not too loud.
- Avoid noise at night and switch off any machinery that is not needed overnight.

- Keep your burglar alarms serviced and make sure that you have made the correct key-holder arrangements.
- Maintain your equipment and make sure that it is fitted with the correct baffles.
- If you have an extra loud bell on your telephone, switch to a soundless telephone with an answerphone at night.

Other nuisance

You may have to monitor other forms of nuisance such as fumes, smoke or dust. Don't wait for someone to take action before you do anything. Buy the correct probes or monitoring devices and use them properly. If there is a problem, deal with it straight away.

Set up systems for ensuring that you don't cause unnecessary nuisance. Store waste, such as dust, that could be spread by the wind, in closed containers. Close all chemical containers when not in use and clean up spills immediately. Water or other liquid seepage can cause significant nuisance to neighbouring premises. Make sure that water systems are turned off at night and especially over holidays or long weekends.

ASSESSING YOUR INPUTS

A typical manufacturing business takes in raw materials for production, materials needed for the day-to-day running of the business, and services such as power and water.

If you haven't done so already, you should gather data on all the materials consumed in your business. You need to know:

- the precise formulation of any chemical or potentially reactive materials
- the quantities of materials in any delivery
- where and how you store materials

- what you do with packaging, pallets or containers

- how materials are loaded and unloaded and if there are any potential risks associated with these procedures (e.g., toxic chemicals unloaded over storm drains could, if the container is ruptured, contaminate a water supply)

- the length of time that you store materials and what risks may arise over time

- whether or not any materials you use contain products extracted from endangered species.

Any business using chemicals needs to examine carefully what happens to these substances while they are in the plant. Owners should assess whether they are in such significant quantities as to pose a risk of a major accident and are thus covered by the Control of Major Accident Hazards Directive. Follow each step in the chemical's journey through your operation and identify where the risks may occur. Apart from major accidents, you should consider:

- Can this material find its way into any waterway through spillage, incorrect disposal or leaks?

- Are containers washed out and what happens to the waste-water involved?

- Who is responsible for disposing of contaminated waste containers?

- What happens to materials contaminated whilst using or cleaning up chemicals (e.g., rags, paper towels, mops, etc.)? Do these pose an environmental risk?

- Is there any risk that children or others may come onto your site and come in contact with waste-containers or materials?

- Could materials contaminate the land on or adjacent to the site?

You should examine ways that you can reduce these risks. Some steps are simpler than others

are. Better housekeeping will eliminate some altogether. More attention to stock management may allow you to reduce the quantity that you store on site and you may also be able to get your supplier to take away your empty containers. Your staff need training in handling materials, not only from a health and safety perspective, but also with regard to their environmental responsibilities.

You should consider isolating environmentally harmful chemicals in a special area or cage. Make sure that this is separated from water and other outlets and that floors and lower walls are sealed against spillage.

Packaging in

The packaging that comes with goods inwards can cause you a waste disposal problem in its own right. Incoming packaging that you dispose of as waste does not count as part of your overall packaging for the purposes of the packaging regulations. It does form part of your waste burden. As such, you look to see how you can minimise, reuse or recycle it in some way.

One step worth exploring is assessing whether or not the goods need as much packaging as they have at present. Most companies over-package to meet the most stringent conditions that the product is likely to encounter. If this level of protection isn't necessary in your case, you could explore the possibility of your supplier using less packaging. This yields a direct saving, as less time will be spent opening, handling and disposing of packaging.

You can reuse some packaging without too much difficulty – pallets are a good example of this. Other containers may also be reused either by your company or by the supplier.

Refill agreements can reduce supply costs.

You should avoid burning packaging wherever possible. Producing dark smoke as described under the air pollution regulation may land you in court (see Chapter 5). If at all possible, you should seek to recycle any waste packaging remaining.

Fuel, energy and water

Treat fuel oils like any other chemical mix. Institute a regular checking programme to identify leaks, rust, wear and tear to the tank, pipes and valves. Common sense suggests that you site oil tanks away from the drainage system and that you position them so that any spillage will be channelled to a place where it is least likely to do damage. Make certain that oil is spills don't get on to roadways or footpaths.

You must have a water abstraction licence to take water from any waterway or an underground reserve. The Environment Agency issues these licences. They may impose conditions and stipulate the quantity you can use or the flow rate. The Agency will charge you a licence fee. You are required to notify the Agency if you take over a licence.

Water is a resource like any other and so you should avoid waste. As with all other systems put a regular monitoring system in place and check piping and valves regularly. Monitor usage to identify any sudden increases that may indicate that there is a problem.

MANAGING YOUR PROCESSES

If you have followed the suggestions in this chapter so far then you will already have addressed many of the issues that may arise concerning your production processes. Every business is different and so faces different environmental challenges. Even within a specific sector, each business is uniquely structured to meet its own market niche. Nevertheless, you may find that others have dealt with many of the issues you may face.

Follow the raw materials through your processes and identify where there are potential environmental impacts. Examine issues such as:

- materials use and waste
- work in progress – how is it stored and does it pose any environmental hazard
- machinery efficiency – water, energy and materials
- transport and movement within the process
- emissions and waste.

POINT TO NOTE

Good managers will recognise that quality control usually results in good environmental management, too. For example, a printing company that reduces overruns caused by failure to meet print quality standards reduces costs, saves paper and cuts down on waste. It saves machine time (an energy-saving, too) and frees up storage space for work in progress. Anyone operating to ISO 9000 series standard or equivalent is well positioned to achieve excellence in environmental performance.

OUTPUTS, INTENTIONAL AND OTHERWISE

Your product is your most important output. There are specific regulations in place or being developed governing a range of products. You should check with your industry sector bodies or the Environment Agency to make sure that you comply with these regulations. New regulations such as WEEE (see Chapter 7) will place increasing constraints on what can or cannot be used and the performance level expected.

Packaging is often the next most important part of your product. You should ensure that you are complying with packaging regulations as well as looking at how you can minimise packaging. Sub-suppliers should discuss their customers' needs as regards packaging. Customers may welcome a less-packaged product or large, economy packs as opposed to regular packs.

You should seek to increase the amount of recycled materials used in your packaging. This is normally cheaper and is well accepted. For example, in some instances you can replace polystyrene with corrugated or 'egg-box' cardboard.

Some companies can reuse their packaging or containers – especially in business-to-business relationships. This takes a little planning and organisation as you have to collect the discarded packaging from your customers. You also have to check the returned items to ensure that they aren't damaged and are suitable for reuse.

Dealing with waste

As we've seen in earlier chapters, waste management is now an essential part of your business. You should identify the different wastes produced and sort them as appropriate for reuse, recycling or disposal. You must pay attention to hazardous, dangerous and special waste, which is treated differently to controlled waste (see Chapter 6).

You must transfer controlled waste to an authorised person such as a registered carrier, a company with a waste-management licence, or a waste collection or disposal authority. You must prepare a note giving relevant information about the waste including:

- who produced the waste and where it was produced
- what particular substances are contained
- how you generated the waste
- the physical and/or chemical composition of the waste
- the quantity of waste involved.

You should label the waste containers with this information as well. You should keep this record and also use it to prepare a transfer note for the person receiving your waste. This should list all of the information above and:

- the type of containers used, or, if the waste is loose, the date and time of the transfer
- your company's address and that of the person taking the waste from you
- whether you are the original producer of the waste or transferring it on
- is the waste recipient authorised to transport this type of waste, together with their category of authorisation or the exemptions that apply.

Keep copies of all of this documentation.

There are different procedures for special waste. The Special Waste Regulation 1996 covers this waste category. It is special waste:

- if it is listed in the appropriate schedule and if it has one of a list of fourteen hazardous properties defined by the regulation
- if it is prescription-only medicine
- if its flashpoint is 21°C (70°F) or below.
- if it is classed as an irritant, toxic, carcinogenic, corrosive or harmful.

If the waste meets any of the above criteria, then you must use the consignment note system. This allows the waste to be tracked as it travels towards final disposal. You must contact the Environment Agency in advance of disposing of such waste. They will advise you on your responsibilities. If you produce waste of this type or are likely to do so in the future and you are uncertain of your responsibilities, you should contact the Agency. Do not mix special or hazardous waste with controlled or other waste. Do not store special waste for any longer than is absolutely necessary.

GOOD ENVIRONMENTAL PRACTICE AND YOUR BUSINESS

You need some structure to make sure that you are managing your environmental responsibilities properly. A number of steps will help you to reach that stage of environmental competence.

Check the regulations

In the first instance, you must decide which regulations apply to your business. Use the earlier part of this chapter and the chapters on the different environmental legislation as a guide. You should also consult the DEFRA and the Environment Agency Netregs websites to help you in this process (see Appendix for full contact details).

Croners Environmental Management Handbook[i] service gives detail on all aspects of the environment and its regulation. They provide monthly updates (printed and on-line) and a newsletter for an annual fee. The Stationery Office publishes the legislation and many other guides and technical documents while publishers such as Butterworths regularly produce collections of statutes relating to the environment.

Assign responsibility for the environment

Nothing ever gets done unless its someone's job to do it. Managing your environmental responsibilities is no different. Give someone overall responsibility and authority for this area. Their role should be to ensure that:

- your company continues to fully comply with current legislation
- you monitor all potential risk areas and have the appropriate safeguards in place
- you record this monitoring and maintenance as well as any incidences that occur
- you keep up to date with legislative changes and proposals
- your staff are properly trained and aware of their environmental responsibilities
- you consider environmental impacts of any changes or developments such as the purchase of a new plant or the introduction of new processes or products.

Business in the Environment (BiE – see Appendix for contact details) produces a range of guides and training manuals for businesses. These will help your environmental officer put the basic systems in place that you need to ensure regulatory compliance.

Make sure that you inform those carrying out contract work on your premises of your environmental procedures. Make compliance to your environmental procedures part of any contract and extend monitoring systems to include contractors on your site.

Keep good records

Develop a series of simple checklists that will allow staff to carry out regular checks and monitoring programmes as appropriate. Make sure that when these inspections happen, they are carried out thoroughly and that any faults or problems are dealt with immediately. File the completed checklists and record any actions taken to rectify problems.

You should record all monitoring results and keep readings for future reference. Keep all records of waste procedures and disposals. Monitor your use of water, fuel and electricity and note what you are using. Review these readings at regular intervals and identify any significant changes in these statistics. Look for explanations of any deviation from the norm.

Make contact with others

You aren't the only company trying to improve their environmental performance. It is most likely that there are others close to you attempting to do the same. Find out if there is a 'Green Business Club' in your area. There are hundreds of these dotted around the country. The local authority or your Chamber of Commerce are most likely to be involved, if not actually running them. The first clubs were established by the Advisory Committee on Business and the Environment (ACBE), a government committee. There are also a number of specialist waste-minimisation groups. For example, Payback in Plymouth established a number of these groups in its area. Each group received training plus direct help from Payback. Companies can expect savings of approximately £1,000 per employee or approximately 1 per cent of turnover.

CARPET MANUFACTURER FLOORS WASTE

Envirowise, a government programme giving environmental advice to business (see Appendix for details), reports that a local waste minimisation scheme helped a carpet manufacturer implement a successful waste-minimisation programme. The company has achieved savings of £46,000 annually with further low-cost savings of £56,000 identified. They have saved over £30,000 a year by reducing the use of high-value material. They reduced solid waste sent to landfill by 50 per cent. Envirowise believes that many other small manufacturing companies could achieve similar savings.

Other organisations such as the Groundwork Trusts now run extensive programmes specifically aimed at SMEs (see Appendix for full contact details). They provide support for business clubs and individual companies. Their services can include organising workshops, waste-minimisation audits, training, software tools and consultant support. They normally offer local helplines. Contact your local business organisations to find out what is happening in your area and what they have to offer. You should also visit the Envirowise site regularly for information on clubs and activities in your area.

WHAT SHOULD YOU DO?

- Review all of your activities.
- Obtain copies of legislation and regulations that apply to your business.
- Take actions to minimise waste and reduce environmental impacts.
- Monitor your environmental impacts systematically with routine checks and reviews.
- Assign responsibility for environmental affairs.
- Train staff so that they can fulfil their environmental responsibilities.
- Make contact with local green business and waste-minimisation clubs.

NOTES TO CHAPTER 7

i   Croner's Environmental Management Service, Croner CCH Group Ltd (first published 1991, updated continuously).

CHAPTER 8

Turning green – beyond compliance

Environmental legislation creates market opportunities – in this chapter we look at how you can position yourself to benefit from them. We cover:

- green business – what it is and the advantages of going green
- green sub-supplying
- Government procurement and green purchasing
- a checklist for going green
- communicating greenness
- how to get the most from environmental consultants
- green business opportunities.

The minimum any company must do is comply with the law. A lot of companies approach their environmental responsibilities in this way – doing the minimum possible and at the latest possible time. This may be bad business practice and, in the long term, be bad for business. In this chapter we explore how a company can take a positive approach to the environment and reap significant rewards as a consequence.

WHAT IS A GREEN BUSINESS?

Green business is best described as a business approach that meets the need of the present without comprising the ability to meet future needs. A green business is one that carries out its operations in a sustainable way.

There are two broad categories of green business. The first category is a traditional business that shifts towards a sustainable development approach. It does its best to minimise its negative environmental impacts and to maximise environmental benefits. The second type of green business is one that offers green products or services, often to other companies, such as: eco-friendly packaging, petrol from waste, environmentally friendly recycling, green consultancy services, and developers of alternative eco-friendly systems and processes. Obviously, there can be an overlap and some companies that have been successful in reducing their environmental impact have graduated to providing an environmental service to other companies.

WHAT ARE THE ADVANTAGES TO GOING GREEN?

Companies can gain tremendously from taking a green approach to their business. And the benefits are directly reflected in the bottom line. For most companies, a greener approach will:

- reduce material costs
- reduce running and maintenance costs
- improve quality and efficiency
- create new marketing opportunities
- improve staff morale
- make financing easier
- develop new business opportunities for products and services
- reduce insurance premia
- create better community and public relations.

BUT I SELL TO OTHER BUSINESSES – THEY DON'T LOOK FOR GREEN CREDENTIALS

Consumers of all shapes and sizes are becoming more green-conscious. Larger corporations are now keen to demonstrate their own green credentials and are putting their own environmental programmes in place. They extend these to their suppliers and increasingly they get their suppliers to match their standards as if they were part of the company itself. For example, McDonald's, the global food-chain states in its commitment to the environment:

'We realise that in today's world, a business leader must be an environmental leader as well. Hence our determination to analyse every aspect of our business in terms of its impact on the environment, and to take actions beyond what is expected if they hold the prospect of leaving future generations an environmentally sound world. We will lead, both in word and in deed.'[ii]

McDonald's spell out specific steps that they take to improve environmental performance, including 'encouraging environmental values and practices'. Dealing with suppliers they state that:

'We intend to continue to work in partnership with our suppliers in the pursuit of these policies. Our suppliers will be held accountable for achieving mutually established waste-reduction goals as well as continuously pursuing sound production practices which minimise environmental impact. Compliance with these policies will receive consideration with other business criteria in evaluating both current and potential McDonald's suppliers.'

Sub-suppliers

Those selling goods to large corporations should take a keen interest in how these customers approach their environmental responsibilities. You should get a copy of each of your customers' environment policies and pay particular attention to what it says about treatment of suppliers and goods purchased. You may find that they have an environmental programme in place with the intention of instituting changes that may have serious implications for your business in the coming years. Larger companies review their suppliers at regular intervals and may implement changes during such a review.

Pay special attention if you supply the local office of a foreign-based multinational. Check out the parent company's environmental plans closely as sometimes these can be introduced by decree with a requirement that supplies meet certain standards after a certain date.

Remember that it doesn't matter where you are in the supply chain. If you produce products or materials that your customer sells on to a corporation it is still in your interest to check out the end-company's environmental policy and standards. If your customer loses the contract because they haven't met the end-customer's standards then you'll both suffer.

Think about modelling your own environmental policy on those of your major customers. You will find it easier to pre-qualify for contracts.

BANKS AND FINANCIAL INSTITUTIONS ALSO CHECK ENVIRONMENTAL CREDENTIALS

Banks want to minimise risk. Now they pay close attention to the possible environmental impact of any company or project that they fund. For example, Deutsche Bank's environmental policy states:

> 'Environmental protection is a key factor in our business policy decision-making. We consider environmental issues when deciding on loans and support our customers in recognising environment-related risks and opportunities.'[i]

This does not mean that banks don't lend to non-green companies but they now examine environmental policies carefully. They are becoming increasingly cautious about lending to or investing in a company that runs the risk of being prosecuted or closed down as a consequence of not adhering to environmental regulations. Banks are also well aware of the general shift towards green business and that a company's market may disappear if its product doesn't meet its customers' environmental standards.

Investors look at all aspects of a business under consideration. They may seek a higher return on capital if they perceive that your company poses an additional risk. There are an increasing number of ethical and green investment funds in the marketplace. These only invest in those meeting their environmental criteria. Poor environmental practice closes off this financing opportunity.

Insurance companies deal in risk. Good environmental practices will be reflected in reduced premiums and more rapid payments on relevant claims.

SUPPLYING GOVERNMENT BODIES – GREEN PROCUREMENT

Government buyers spend approximately £25 billion annually. When Government decides to apply green criteria when purchasing, it can have a very big impact on current and potential suppliers.

Current Government procurement policy insists on official buyers getting value for money (vfm) when purchasing goods and services. This doesn't mean purchasing at the lowest price. In fact, it aims to achieve the best value for money based on the whole-life costs of the product and the appropriate quality for its purpose.

For Government buyers, this means assessing:

* maintenance and running costs (power and water usage)
* indirect costs (e.g., additional burden on air-conditioning systems caused by less energy-efficient IT equipment)
* administrative costs such as health and safety issues associated with hazardous materials
* disposal costs and future trends in landfill taxes that may increase the overall disposal costs.

The Government has produced a green guide for its buyers covering the policy and practices governing purchasing. It stresses the three Rs of reduce, reuse and recycle. It also adds an additional R, standing for rethinking. This means re-examining purchases to see if the buyer can achieve the same result using a different approach. The green procurement website gives a good example of what this means in practice:

'The National Demand Management Centre could have fitted urinal flush controls at their headquarters as the obvious choice to save water. Instead, they chose to buy and install waterless urinals which have reduced water consumption by nearly 60 per cent and saved £2,250 in the first year.'

The UK Government has moved rapidly down the green procurement road. The European Union also applies similar criteria. Other governments are following. So, if you hope to break into or stay in the lucrative public supplies market, you should check your product's green credentials. The checklist in the accompanying box should prove of help in this regard.

TURNING YOUR BUSINESS GREEN

This checklist was prepared by Jan-Olaf Willums with the World Business Council for Sustainable Development in 'The Sustainable Business Challenge: a Briefing for Tomorrow's Business Leaders'.[iii] The Government's green procurement website reproduces it. The list helps you to become more environmentally effective and thus improve your competitive performance.

Material intensity

✔ Can the product or services be redesigned to make less use of material outputs? ❑

✔ Are there less intensive raw materials? ❑

✔ Can raw materials be produced or processed in less material-intensive ways? ❑

✔ Would higher quality materials create less waste in later stages? ❑

✔ Can water, waste-water treatment or waste disposal costs be allocated to budgets to encourage greater control? ❑

✔ Can yields be increased by better maintenance, control and other means? ❑

✔ Can waste be utilised for other uses? ❑

✔ Can products be made smaller or a different shape to minimise use of material and packaging? ❑

✔ Can packaging be eliminated or reduced? ❑

Energy

✔ Can raw materials be produced with less or renewable energy? ❑

✔ Would substitute materials or components reduce the overall energy intensity? ❑

✔ Can energy costs be directly allocated to budgets to encourage better control? ❑

✔ Can energy be exchanged between processes or can waste heat be re-used? ❑

✔ Can process energy or the energy consumption of buildings be better monitored? ❑

✔ Could better maintenance improve energy efficiency? ❑

✔ Is there scope for better energy housekeeping, e.g., energy-efficient lighting? ❑

✔ Can the product or service be combined with others to reduce overall energy intensity? ❑

✔ Can the energy efficiency of products in use be improved? ❑

✔ Can transport be reduced or greater use be made of energy-efficient transport? ❑

✔ Are there incentives for employees to cycle or use public transport or car pools? ❑

Toxic Dispersion

✔ Can toxic dispersion be reduced or eliminated using alternative materials or different processes? ❑

✔ Are products designed to ensure their safe distribution, use and disposal? ❑

✔ Can harmful substances be eliminated from production processes? ❑

✔ Can harmful substances generated in use be reduced or eliminated?

✔ Can any remaining harmful substances be recycled or incinerated? ❑

✔ Are remaining harmful substances properly handled during production and dispersal? ❑

✔ Are equipment and vehicles properly maintained so that emissions are kept to a minimum? ❑

Recyclability

✔ Can the product be re-used, remanufactured or recycled? ❏

✔ Can wastes from raw material production be re-used or recycled? ❏

✔ Would separation of waste streams make recycling easier or reduce costs? ❏

✔ Can product specification be modified to enable greater use of recycled materials or components? ❏

✔ Can products be made of marked, easily recycled materials? ❏

✔ Can products be designed to facilitate customer revalorisation? ❏

✔ Can products be designed for easy disassembly? ❏

✔ Can product packaging be made re-usable or more recyclable? ❏

✔ Can old products and components be remanufactured or reused? ❏

✔ Are there opportunities to participate in waste-exchange schemes? ❏

✔ Can products be made biodegradable or harmless so that less energy is required for disposal? ❏

Durability

✔ Can materials or processes be altered to improve longevity? ❏

✔ Can products or components be made more modular to allow easy upgrading? ❏

✔ Can whatever aspects of the product that limit durability be redesigned? ❏

✔ Can maintenance of the product be improved? ❏

✔ Can customers be informed of ways to extend product durability? ❏

Service intensity

✔ What are customers really getting from your product? ❏

✔ Can this be provided more effectively or in a completely different way? ❏

✔ What service will customers need in the future? ❏

✔ Can you design new or develop existing products to meet them? ❏

✔ Is your product improving other services as well as the most obvious one? ❏

✔ Can it be integrated/synchronised with others to provide multifunctionality? ❏

✔ Can customers' disposal problems be eliminated by providing a take-back service? ❏

✔ Can production be localised both to enhance service and reduce transport needs? ❏

PUTTING THE ELEMENTS IN PLACE

Becoming a greener company requires commitment and initial effort if you are to achieve results. The checklist included in this chapter should guide you through the process.

Most companies start off by developing an environmental policy stating their approach to the environment. This is a general document and is used for both internal and external audiences. It can help motivate staff and increase environmental awareness while externally it makes your customers and the general public aware of your environmental commitment.

People Seating Limited is an example of a small business supplying some of the top names in the transportation sector. It is a competitive and changing marketplace where companies have to compete across a range of factors including price, quality, delivery and the environment. Their policy:

- commits the company to operating its business in an environmentally responsible way
- fully meets its regulatory requirements
- implements measures aimed at improving performance in specific areas of its operation
- communicates its policy to its customers and the public.

PEOPLE SEATING LIMITED ENVIRONMENTAL POLICY[vi]

People Seating Limited recognises the importance of environmental protection and is committed to operating its business responsibly and in compliance with all environmental regulations, legislation and approved codes of practice relating to the commercial and industrial seating industry and the activities of this Company. It is the Company's objective to operate with, and to maintain good relations with, all regulatory bodies.

It is the declared policy of People Seating Limited to carry out all measures reasonably practicable to meet, exceed or develop all necessary or desirable requirements and to continually improve environmental performance through implementation of the following:

- assessment and regular re-assessment of the environmental effects of the Company's activities
- assessment and regular re-assessment of the Company's environmental objects and targets
- training of all employees and management in environmental issues
- minimisation of the production of waste
- minimisation of material wastage
- minimisation of energy wastage
- promotion of the use of recyclable and renewable materials
- reduction and/or limitation of the production of pollutants to water, land and air
- control of noise emissions from operations
- minimisation of the risk to the general public and employees from operations and activities undertaken by the Company.

This policy is communicated to all employees, suppliers and sub-contractors and is made available to the public.

AUDITING YOUR PERFORMANCE

A formal policy allows you to set the parameters within which you will operate. An environmental audit enables you to systematically examine your business operations and determine their impacts upon the environment. You can compare an environmental audit to a financial audit. Like a financial audit, the environmental audit looks at all of your practices, products and outcomes and quantifies weaknesses in the system. It gives you a snapshot of your environmental performance – usually against agreed industry or other standards. As with the financial audit, you now have a quantified, statistical basis for your environmental performance.

An audit should examine barriers to effective policy implementation such as communication and training. An environmental policy needs to be communicated regularly and updated frequently. Your staff must understand it and be skilled in its implementation. In addition, an audit will examine:

- regulatory and standards compliance
- strategic alignment, i.e., that your environmental policy is integrated with your overall business strategy
- costs and benefits
- specific issues and products, e.g., energy, waste, raw materials, etc.
- product life-cycle and disposal including value for money
- premises and environs.

The audit is only complete when you prepare a report on its findings and communicate these to the appropriate stakeholders. Some corporate customers may want copies of such reports. You should present the findings to staff and consider making results that aren't commercially sensitive available to the wider public through the world-wide-web.

MAKING THE BEST USE OF OUTSIDE HELP

SMEs normally don't have the depth and range of skills necessary to deal with all environmental issues using their own resources. Sometimes it's necessary to draw on external personnel to boost the internal team. Companies can be put off by the prospect of hiring consultants to help them. You don't always have to hire consultants and with careful planning it should be possible to reduce the amount of consultancy time needed.

There are organisations that may give you help for nothing or at a reduced rate. You should check out organisations such as Envirowise and the Groundworks Trust and establish what they can offer your company. For example, Envirowise offers free, independent advice, site visits, events and publications. You should check out the Envirowise and Groundworks websites (see the Appendix for contact details) to find out about activities in your area.

There are others who may be able to help you to improve your environmental performance. Some large corporate institutions give help and advice to their SME suppliers and may have programmes in place to bring those suppliers up to their environmental standards. Your bank or financial institution may also have programmes in place aimed at improving their business customers' environmental performance. It is well worth exploring these avenues as, if nothing else, they demonstrate your commitment to improving your environmental performance to both customers and investors.

Using consultants

In some cases you will need to use consultants' services. Good planning will ensure that you get the maximum return on this investment. Use your local business networks to get the names of consultants that have worked with similarly sized companies to your own and who have experience of your industry sector.

The Environmental Data Service (ENDS – refer to the Appendix for full details) publishes a directory of environmental consultants. Local directories, business and trade associations will also have the names of consultants in your area.

Ascertain the following when recruiting consultants:

- their knowledge of the regulations that apply generally and in your sector
- the individual that will work with your company and how they will fit in with you and your workforce
- the names of previous companies that they have worked with (get permission to contact these to validate their experience)
- their fee structure and what is or isn't included
- the amount of your time and that of your employees that they draw upon when they are working in your plant
- whether or not they will need office space on your premises
- the output that they will deliver
- other costs, such as laboratory analysis or materials testing, that might be incurred.

Establish a clear reporting structure for the consultants working with you. Give them guidance about who they may talk to within the company. You should alert your customers if your consultants wish to contact them. It is useful to assign someone to work with or shadow the consultants. It is a form of training and will introduce your staff to the skills and knowledge that they need. Your own personnel may be able to take over the consultant's role at a later stage.

BLOWING YOUR GREEN TRUMPET

Publicising your company's environmental achievements is good for business. Customers like to know that you are doing your bit and the community generally looks favourably on companies that present a positive environmental image. A green image can be of tremendous practical benefit. It may help to reduce potential objections to development if the community perceive you as contributing to the environment. It can be the clinching factor in sales and it attracts new recruits and helps to motivate those already working with you.

You should include an environmental section in your company's annual report. Some businesses produce a separate environmental report. You can distribute these reports to customers, suppliers, staff and the local community. If you do produce such a report, you should make sure that you make copies available to local libraries, schools and colleges, resident groups and associations, the local authority, local media and other local influencers.

An environmental report can vary from a short statement to a comprehensive presentation of your entire business and its interactions with the environment. A good environmental report addresses the following issues:

- your environmental policy
- significant environmental impacts
- products, their life-cycle and their impacts
- energy consumption
- waste management
- transportation and travel
- benchmarking against others and standards
- future plans and developments.
- independent verification (where you have obtained it).

Regardless of what you include in the report, make sure that you produce the report itself in an environmentally friendly manner. Use recycled paper and, where possible, printers with a recognised commitment to the environment. You can also make it available on the world-wide-web (a cheaper and potentially more environmentally friendly option).

Your brochures and promotional literature should refer to your environmental policy and practices. Consider giving environmental information on labels or packaging – particularly if you produce consumer products. Make sure that sales staff understand what you are doing for the environment and that they incorporate this information into their sales pitches where appropriate.

Green claims code

The Government launched a code of practice governing businesses' environmental claims. It is supported by the Confederation of British Industry, the British Retail Consortium, the local authorities' co-ordinating body on food and trading standards, and the British Standards Institution. The current code takes account of the ISO 14021 standard governing environmental claims.

The code describes a green claim as information, either text, symbols or graphics, appearing on a product, its packaging or in related literature or in advertising which makes a claim about its environmental aspects. The code does not consider straightforward advice (e.g., how to dispose of a product) as an environmental claim. Such advice should still be realistic.

Some sectors have their own legal labelling requirements, e.g., foodstuffs, pharmaceuticals and hazardous materials, but the code still covers additional voluntary environmental claims about these products.

The code sets down certain principles for environmental claims. They should be:

- *Truthful, accurate, and able to be substantiated*. This may require that you test the product to substantiate the claim. You must keep adequate records of these and other checks and you must be prepared to give the relevant information to anyone asking for it.

- *Relevant.* The claim must relate to the product directly. The code points out that it is misleading to say that a paper was made without using tropical hardwood when such materials are not normally used to make paper.

- *Clear.* The claim should be clear and it should be obvious what part of the product it refers to. Don't make claims for an entire product that apply only to a certain part.

- *Symbols must have a clear meaning.* Symbols too must meet the same standards as the printed word. If you have your own symbol, you must explain clearly what it means. Only use symbols from other organisations when you are fully satisfied that you are entitled to do so. Don't use symbols to imply endorsement by a standards body when you haven't a right to such a claim.

- *Write your claims in plain language.* Don't allow any exaggeration or ambiguity to creep into your description. If something is 75 per cent, recyclable say so and not 'recyclable.' Avoid vague terms such 'low energy consumption' or 'eco-friendly' in your claims as these are hard to substantiate.

The code also warns against general comparisons or vacuous claims. 'This product outperforms all others in energy efficiency and water consumption' is a hard claim to substantiate.

Don't use environmental claims to suggest that your product is exceptional when it isn't. For example, stating that 'this product uses no water' when none of its competitors do either, deceives the customer.

Trading Standards Officers have powers under the Trade Descriptions Act to act against those making demonstrably false or misleading claims. The Director General of Fair Trading can act under the Control of Misleading Advertisement Regulations 1998. The Advertising Standards Authority, the Independent Television Commission and the Radio Authority administer the appropriate advertising codes for advertising.

GREEN BUSINESSES

Increasing concern for the environment and the need to find solutions to environmental problems has created a whole range of new business opportunities. These businesses are primarily focused on environmental products and services and have developed as a consequence of changing attitudes and legislation. Companies have identified a niche that they can fill. Opportunities range from producing biodegradable plastic bags to the manufacture of bio-fuels. Certain areas have grown significantly – particularly those relating to waste management, recycling and disposal.

BEACON PRESS – A SHINING EXAMPLE[v]

Based in Uckfield, East Sussex, Beacon Press has built a reputation for environmental awareness and has received 15 environmental awards in the last 10 years.

A significant outcome of the company's commitment to sound environmental practices is the pureprint® process. Pureprint® is a proprietary printing system designed to minimise environmental impact whilst increasing quality. The Design Council awarded millennium product status to this innovation.

A key component of pureprint® is the move to waterless printing. This makes more efficient use of raw materials to cut costs, improve quality and reduce environmental impact.

Conventional, alcohol-damped printing plates use dampening solution, composed of water, isopropyl alcohol (IPA) and fountain additives. The solution is applied to printing plates to keep non-printed areas clean and free from ink. Waterless printing eliminates the need for dampening solution. Instead, plates are covered with an ink-repellent silicon rubber layer, parts of which are removed, either by chemical development or by a computer-to-plate process, to reveal the printing area.

Beacon Press started the switch over to waterless printing in July 1995. To offset capital costs, the move was undertaken gradually, with waterless presses only bought to replace spent traditional presses, and was completed in February 1999.

The benefits of the move have already become obvious. Beacon Press was already using a low-alcohol fountain dampening process that required reduced IPA, but the waterless system has eliminated IPA use altogether. Compared with traditional dampening systems, this is equivalent to a saving of 14,300 litres of IPA.

Waterless printing has helped Beacon Press to eliminate waste at source. Under the conventional wet plate system, the company produced 50 litres of spent developer and 50 litres of finishing gum waste every week. Now Beacon's total weekly effluent waste amounts to only around two litres of spent dye solution and waste-water. Water use and disposal has been greatly reduced and, by 1998, the company's annual water consumption had dropped by 26 cubic metres.

Waterless printing also delivers efficiency and quality benefits. For instance, paper wastage at Beacon Press has been reduced by 30 per cent, from 12.2 per cent per job to 8.5 per cent, whilst reduced press downtime has increased capacity. At the same time, Beacon's new system delivers sharper images and improved print quality.

The development of pureprint® and the move to waterless printing has provided Beacon Press with a genuine marketing and sales edge. And because the new technology delivers efficiency and cost savings, the development is paying for itself.

Environmental business opportunities are set to grow further. Current Government spending plans have set aside significant money to support areas such as alternative energy development. These research and development efforts will lead to the development of whole new business sectors. For example, the changes in the tax treatment of energy will shift the balance towards alternative energy sources. It also creates the space necessary for new entrants into the sector.

Environmental businesses are not simply centred on products. Eco-friendly businesses can operate by changing business processes. For example, some companies have switched from a central location to teleworking with staff no longer having to travel. Others have moved a considerable proportion of their business on to the world-wide-web reducing resource consumption.

Environmental consultancy is growing steadily. This includes services centred on:

- carrying out audits and helping companies comply with regulations
- process re-engineering and systems analysis
- new product design
- waste reduction and elimination
- energy consumption
- market identification and analysis
- sourcing environmentally friendly raw materials.

As previously mentioned, waste management is one of the important green businesses. Current legislation ensures that the demand for recycling will increase significantly over the next two decades (this refers to traditional waste materials and also waste generated from the new economy such as redundant computers and telecommunications equipment).

TURNING WASTE INTO PRECIOUS METALS

Precious Metal Industries (PMI) was established in 1986. It specialises in recovering precious metals from electronic and electrical equipment, e.g., printed circuit boards. It carries out sampling and assaying to recover both precious and base metals such as high-grade gold refining.

The company also offers a complete resale and recycling service for IT products and point of sale equipment. They will assess its suitability for reuse. They also repair and refurbish equipment.

The company now has a turnover of £5 million and employs 40 staff. It has an annual throughput of 3,500 tonnes.

ASSESSING YOUR OWN BUSINESS OPPORTUNITIES

Is there an unfilled niche in your business sector or could you convert your current business to a restructured environmentally friendly one? This is a growth area with enormous potential but also with potential risks. As with any other business venture, you need to assess the market, its potential and the costs involved. Some useful steps towards identifying business opportunities include:

1. Assessing your sector – does it use more energy, water or raw materials than other industry sectors?

2. Has your sector remained relatively stable over the past two decades?

3. Is there a market for more environmentally friendly products or services and will this offer a greater margin?

4. Are there barriers to entry that will prevent other environmental businesses moving into the sector?

5. Are there capital cost barriers that prevent larger companies in the sector changing but don't affect new entrants or SMEs?

6. Will proposed regulations affect the traditional industry's cost-base and can you re-engineer to avoid these?

7. Are there Government or other supports available that would reduce the financial risk associated with change?

8. Have you got the personal and financial resources necessary to bring about successful change?

If you answer yes to some of the above, then maybe there's a business opportunity waiting to be exploited.

NOTES TO CHAPTER 9

i   http://www.mcdonalds.com/

ii   Deutsche Bank website. http://www.db.com/.

iii   'The Sustainable Business Challenge: a Briefing for Tomorrow's Business Leaders', Greenleaf Publishing Ltd, 1998 (Reproduced by kind permission of the publisher).

iv   Courtesy of People Seating Limited.

v   Reproduced courtesy of Envirowise. http://www.envirowise.gov.uk/; tel. 0800 585794

vi   Personal communication from Precious Metal Industries.

CHAPTER 9

Getting accreditation

Having an authoritative body validate your environmental claims can boost your business. In this chapter, we look at the following ways in which your product or company can achieve official recognition:

- EMAS – what it is and how to get accredited
- ISO 14000 series – an international set of standards and guidelines
- Project Acorn – an opportunity for SMEs
- Eco-labelling – a clear sign that your product is environmentally friendly.

Improving your environmental management may not be enough to convince your customers that you are eco-friendly. They may want to see your claims verified independently. You too may prefer to know that you are performing to internationally accepted standards and that you are keeping up with the best in terms of environmental performance.

Here, we look at two environmental standards-based accreditation schemes, EMAS and the ISO14000 series, that focus on environmental management. We also give you information on the European eco-label scheme that relates to products.

WHAT IS A STANDARD?

The British Standards Institute (BSI),[i] the UK standards body, defines a standard as a document, established by consensus and approved by a recognised body, that provides, for common and repeated use, rules, guidelines or characteristics for activities or their results. Most companies already operate a range of different standards in areas such as product specification, quality control, health and safety, accounting and so on.

ENVIRONMENTAL MANAGEMENT SYSTEMS (EMS)[ii]

The European Union (EU) introduced a scheme entitled 'Allowing Voluntary

Participation by Companies in the Industrial Sector in a Community Eco-Management and Audit System' in July 1993. It was subsequently adopted as a regulation (93/1836) that the UK Government brought into force in 1995. The scheme is commonly known as EMAS. The EU's aim is to shift from a command and control approach to one that puts greater emphasis on self-regulation.

EMAS is a voluntary environmental management scheme and is based on harmonised lines and principles throughout the European Union. Originally, it was open to companies in the industrial sector only. However, a new EU regulation is extending the scope of EMAS to all organisations operating in the European Union and the European Economic Area (EEA). EMAS had already been extended to local authorities in the UK (LA-EMAS) and also to sites in the distribution sector.

The scheme's purpose is to promote continuous environmental performance improvement by getting applicant companies to make a commitment to:

- evaluate and improve their environmental performance at site level
- provide relevant information to the public.

POINTS TO NOTE ABOUT EMAS

- EMAS is open to businesses in the EU and EEA.
- The scheme is independently verified.
- It applies to specified sites as opposed to whole companies (e.g., if your company operates at different sites, then each site is treated separately).
- You must agree to make non-commercially sensitive environmental information available to the public.
- The new regulation extends the scope beyond industrial to all companies.
- The new regulation emphasises the need for SMEs to become involved in EMAS.
- It is possible now to use the EMAS logo more flexibly to raise your profile, e.g., in advertising and promotional activities. The logo meets the green code requirements.
- EMAS does not replace existing EU or national legislation or technical standards.
- It does not remove a company's obligations under law.

EMAS – HOW IT WORKS

Any company wishing to achieve EMAS accreditation must set up an environmental management system. This identifies all the activities on a site that may have a significant environmental impact. It puts in place a system to manage and control these properly. The company prepares an environmental statement that describes the environmental impact and how it's managed. The statement must be clear and understandable by the public. An independent verifier checks the statement and ensures that the site meets all of the EMAS scheme's requirements. You can only apply to the Competent Body for registration once you have completed these steps.

91

The eight steps to EMAS registration

These are the eight steps you must complete to achieve EMAS accreditation.

1. Prepare an Environmental Policy that sets out the business's environmental priorities and that includes a commitment to comply with the relevant environmental legislation and to continuously improve your site's environmental performance.

2. Review the site's current environmental performance including waste management, raw materials use, energy and water consumption. Identify, in the review, how the site management may improve performance.

3. Prepare an Environmental Programme containing specific objectives and targets for improving the site's environmental performance.

4. Put an Environmental Management System, such as ISO 140001 (discussed later in this chapter), in place.

5. Conduct regular audits and check performance against objectives set in your programme.

6. Prepare a concise environmental statement setting out the environmental performance of the site and explaining how the site's environmental impacts are being managed.

7. Have an independent verifier validate your system and policy. They will confirm that the information is correct and the scheme meets the requirements of EMAS.

8. Send a completed application form, your validated environmental statement, and an application to the EMAS Competent Body so that your site can be registered.

Sites are registered once the Competent Body receives the information listed in point number eight, above, and is satisfied that the site meets the EMAS regulation's requirements including complying with relevant environmental legislation.

Your site can be de-registered if:

• You fail to submit a validated environmental statement and registration fee within three months of the specified deadline.

• If the Competent Body becomes aware that the site no longer complies with the EMAS regulation's requirements

• If an enforcement authority informs a Competent Body that the site no longer complies with relevant environmental legislation.

If you are de-registered, it can only be reversed when the enforcement authority has assured the Competent Body that you have rectified the breaches and that you have put procedures in place to ensure that the problems do not re-occur.

The Official Journal of the European Communities publishes a list of all the registered sites in the 15 Member States plus the EEA countries. These are also available on the world-wide-web and the UK sites are available through the Competent Body in the UK.

EMAS DELIVERS RAPID PAYBACK

A UK bronze- and copper-powder manufacturer, employing 260 staff, has successfully registered under EMAS.[iii] The company incurred costs in three main areas when achieving certification. These were:

1. design, implementation and certification costs

2. early maintenance and surveillance costs

3. capital and labour costs of the EMS including costs associated with controlling significant impacts.

The company also achieved savings in three areas:

1. reduction in wastes needing disposal

2. more efficient use of raw materials and consumables

3. increased energy efficiency.

The company also identified a number of environmental improvements including:

- reduced waste volume to landfill
- improved effluent quality
- reduced volatile organic compound emissions
- legislative compliance (Duty of Care requirements)
- improved relations with stakeholders.

The company estimated that EMAS had a five-month payback period.

WHO DOES WHAT IN EMAS AND HOW DO I FIND THEM?

EMAS has a Competent Body in each EU member state. This is an independent and neutral organisation responsible for the establishment of procedures to organise registration of sites and their suspension or deletion from the register if necessary. There is an accreditation body responsible for accrediting the bodies that verify your site and application. The United Kingdom Accreditation Service (UKAS) is the UK accreditation body. There are approximately 15 individuals or organisations accredited as verifiers in the UK at the time of writing.

The UK Competent Body is the Institute of Environmental Management and Assessment. To register your site for EMAS, or a local authority unit under LA-EMAS, you must have your EMAS environmental statement validated by an independent verifier. You must also complete the appropriate EMAS application form. You then send the validated environmental statement, the completed application form and the registration fee to the Competent Body (address at the end of this chapter).

ISO – A WORLDWIDE STANDARD

The International Organisation for Standardisation (ISO) is a worldwide, non-governmental standards organisation with national members from over 140 countries. Established in 1947, ISO's mission is to promote the development of standardisation and related activities in the world with a view to facilitating the international exchange of goods and services, and to developing co-operation in the spheres of intellectual, scientific, technological and economic activity. Harmonised standards allow for the freer trade in goods and services. It helps overcome barriers to trade. Exporting companies can find international standards such as those set by ISO, a cost-effective way of gaining international recognition for, and acceptance of, their product or service.

Why ISO is not equal to IOS

People are sometimes perplexed by ISO and assume that it is an inaccurate acronym for International Organisation for Standardisation. In fact, ISO is derived from the Greek word 'ISOS' meaning 'equal'. It is easy to make the jump from equal to standard and so it was chosen as the organisation's name.

Most companies are familiar with the ISO 9000 standards for quality assurance. Buyers in major companies often use it as a prerequisite for supplying goods or services. Companies use ISO 9000 as evidence of their commitment to quality.

ISO has developed a series of standards and guidelines for environmental management and these are known as the ISO 14000 series. ISO 14001 is the certifiable standard while the remainder are supporting guidelines. One of the biggest advantages of ISO 14000 registration is that you can use the symbol on your company literature and stationery as clearly demonstrating you have an environmental management system in place and that you are committed to helping create a better environment.

EMAS AND ISO

ISO 14001 was introduced in 1996 and initially had a wider scope than EMAS. ISO is an internationally recognised standard and so companies and governments around the world are familiar with the ISO approach and methodology. EMAS obviously operates in the EU and EEA. The EU does not see the standards as being in competition but instead as emphasising different aspects of environmental management. Increasingly, the EU takes account of ISO 14000 in developing EMAS to reduce or eliminate unnecessary duplication.

The EU cites the following differences between the two schemes:[iv]

- Preliminary review: EMAS requires an initial review.
- Register of effects: ISO 14001 does not require a register of environmental effects or legislation.
- Public availability: EMAS requires that the policy, programme, environmental management system and details of the sites performance are made publicly available as part of the environmental statement. ISO requires that the policy be publicly available.
- Audits: ISO 14001 requires audits, although the frequency is not specified, nor is the audit methodology set out in as much detail as EMAS.
- Contractors, suppliers: the level of control of these bodies required in EMAS is not matched in ISO 14001, which requires only that required procedures are communicated to them.
- Commitments and requirements: employee involvement, continuous improvement of environmental performance and compliance with legislation are an integral part of EMAS. ISO 14001 does not stipulate the extent to which performance

must be improved. EMAS specifies that companies must attempt to 'reduce environmental impacts to levels not exceeding those corresponding to the economically viable application of the best available technology'.

Companies should choose the standard that most closely meets their particular needs. If you have an ISO series standard already, then you may prefer to continue with a system that you are used to. ISO is recognised internationally and this may influence your decision. ISO may be more convenient if you operate a number of sites.

WHAT ARE THE ISO 14000 STANDARDS AND GUIDELINES?

There is one standard with supporting guidelines. These are[v]:

ISO 14001: 1996, Environmental management systems – specification with guidance for use. This international standard helps you to establish an Environmental Management System. It applies to environmental aspects that the organisation can control and influence. ISO 14001 replaced BS 7750 in the UK in June 1997.

ISO 14004: 1996, Environmental management systems – general guidelines on principles, systems and supporting techniques. This gives additional guidance on developing and maintaining an environmental management system including practical help sections.

ISO 14010: 1996, Guidelines for environmental auditing – general principles.

ISO 14011: 1996, Guidelines for environmental auditing – Audit procedures – Auditing environmental management systems.

ISO 14020: 1998, Environmental labels and declarations – General principles. This guidance document establishes nine principles for the development and use of environmental labels and declarations.

ISO 14021: 1999, Environmental labels and declarations – Environmental labelling TYPE II. This forms the basis for the Green Claims Code that provides users with a basic summary of this type of environmental labelling.

ISO 14024: 1999, Environmental labels and declarations – Environmental Labelling TYPE III.

ISO 14032: 1999, Technical Report – Case studies illustrating the use of ISO 14031.

ISO 14040: 1997, Environmental management life-cycle assessment – Principles and framework.

ISO 14041: 1998, Environmental management life-cycle assessment – Life-cycle inventory analysis.

ISO 14050: 1998, Environmental management vocabulary. This document contains definitions, in English and French, of fundamental concepts relating to environmental management used in ISO 14000 standards: BS EN ISO14001, BS ISO 14004, BS EN ISO 14004, BS EN ISO 14010, BS EN ISO 14011, BS EN ISO 14012.

ISO Guide 64: Guide for the inclusion of environmental aspects in production standards – The definitive guide for standards writers wishing to take the environment into account when developing product standards.

HOW DO I GET ISO CERTIFICATION?

The British Standards Institution (BSI) is the British standards body for ISO. It is the oldest standards body of its type in the world and offers a wide range of standards-related services.

BSI lays out five easy steps for developing an environmental management system leading to ISO 14001 certification. (See diagram from page 101.)

BSI will help EU-based companies register to the sixth stage of EMAS verification under the EU EMAS regulation. This relates to the registration of specific sites rather than the whole organisation. As noted earlier, EMAS requires the publication and validation of a public environmental statement by an independent accredited verifier. BSI can verify that you meet EMAS requirements. They can validate your environmental statement, check the system and internal audit programme. They can also offer simultaneous certification to ISO 14001 and verification to EMAS. We include BSI's contact details at the end of this chapter.

PROJECT ACORN – A SPECIAL PROGRAMME FOR SMES

Project Acorn is a two-year pilot programme that was launched at the end of 2000. It takes a different approach to developing and certifying standards. The project aims to work with large companies and their SME suppliers to develop mutually beneficial environmental management programmes. DTI is grant-aiding the project to support companies through the EMS implementation process and to help train nominated employees in the use of environmental management tools and systems.

The project gives SMEs the opportunity to develop environmental management systems in a way that matches their overall business development. In addition, by bringing both customers and suppliers together during the process, it creates an extra bond that in itself is good for business. It takes a five-level approach to implementing an environmental management system. In a sixth, reporting level, companies may register for EMAS.

SMEs have access to:
- modular training
- a telephone help-line
- consultancy support
- documentation
- a handbook specifically developed to help SMEs navigate through the EMS implementation process.

Companies also have the option of gaining modular certification at each level. This will ultimately lead to ISO 14001 certification and/or registration to EMAS.

The project provides a framework for the systematic management of environmental issues within individual companies and the supply chains to which they belong. The project uses indicators and performance evaluation techniques based on ISO 14031 to monitor environmental performance over time. It gives companies evidence of their progress and allows them to address issues in a planned and phased way.

Project Acorn uses a model based on ISO 14001. In addition, the project is developing Environmental Protection Indicators (EPIs) that are more closely matched to the SMEs needs than more traditional measures. The model's six levels are:

1. Top management committing to the project, conducting an initial environmental review, and initiating culture change to support the concept of continual performance improvement.

2. Meeting legal, customer and market requirements.

3. Confirming and managing significant environmental aspects and impacts.

4. Launching an effective EMS.

5. Checking, auditing and reviewing.

6. Data verification, public reporting and EMAS registration.

Companies can enter the model at any level – provided that they can prove that they have already completed the earlier levels. Some companies, such as micro-companies, may prefer not to put a full EMS in place. In this situation, companies can choose to stay at a specific level and not progress to a full ISO 14001 system.

The project will be disseminated more widely after the pilot phase.

Who is Project Acorn for?

Project Acorn is targeting two groups of companies:

1. Mentors: larger companies that have a track record in environmental initiatives including registering to ISO 14001 or EMAS, but who now need to address environmental impacts arising from their supply chain. They are now looking for an environmental management model that suits all parties and will deliver overall gains.

2. SMEs who want to improve their environmental performance and have the support of one key customer willing to act as a mentor.

THE EUROPEAN ECO-LABEL SCHEME – HARNESSING CONSUMER POWER

Consumer pressure is one way of putting pressure on manufacturers to produce more environmentally friendly products. If consumers select eco-friendly products in preference to others, then these producers will flourish at the expense of the less eco-friendly competitors. While this is fine in theory, in reality consumers have not been able to reconcile conflicting claims for competing products. Consumers have become cynical, believing that some companies are introducing cosmetic changes to allow them to present their activities as 'green'.

The EU recognised that there was a strong need to harness consumer choice as a force for environmental improvement. It devised and developed the EU eco-labelling scheme and the Council of Ministers agreed it in December 1991. The Regulation, which came into effect in the following year, established a voluntary eco-label scheme intended to:

• promote the design, production, marketing and use of products that have a reduced environmental impact during their entire life-cycle

• provide consumers with better information on the environmental impact of products.

The scheme fits in with the EU's use of market-based instruments as a means of improving the environment. The scheme has had limited success to date, but a review in the late 1990s followed by a new regulation in 2000 widened the scheme and enhanced its potential impact.

THE NEW EU ECO-LABEL REGULATION

In September 2000, a new eco-label regulation replaced the original 1992 one. The new regulation improves the scheme and also makes it easier for SMEs to be awarded eco-labels for their products. The key elements of the new regulation are:

- it now covers services as well as products
- greater stakeholder participation, in particular in the development of environmental criteria
- the creation of the EU Eco-labelling Board (EUEB), comprising of the eco-label competent bodies and interest groups, whose main role is to develop the eco-label criteria
- reduced fees for SMEs and developing countries
- introduction of a ceiling on the annual fee
- reinforced transparency and methodology
- renewed emphasis on the promotion of the scheme
- reinforced co-operation and co-ordination with national eco-label schemes
- more information on the label
- trader and retailers may apply for the eco-label for own-brand products
- non-EU producers have the possibility of applying directly.

THE MAIN ELEMENTS OF THE ECO-LABEL SCHEME[vi]

A selective approach....

The scheme only awards labels to products with the lowest environmental impact in a product range. Product categories are carefully defined so that all products that have direct 'equivalence of use' from the consumers' perspective are included in the same product category. For example, a study of possible eco-label criteria for rubbish bags is examining both paper and plastic bags.

That is transparent....

Industry representatives, commercial bodies, trade unions, environmental and consumer organisations all have an input into the eco-label scheme. The new regulation strengthened this participation through the creation of the EU Eco-labelling Board (EUEB) that brings a range of different perspectives, both commercial and consumer, to the revised scheme.

Using a multi-criteria approach...

The scheme adopts an entire life-cycle approach when analysing a product's impact on the environment. The assessment can start with the extraction of raw materials, examination of pre-production stages, production, distribution, product use and its final disposal.

With a European dimension....

A manufacturer who is awarded the right to use the eco-label can market his eco-labelled products throughout all the member states of the EU, and also in the countries that are signatories of the EEA Agreement (Norway, Iceland and Liechtenstein). The same logo will be used regardless of the product group thereby eliminating consumer confusion.

Voluntary participation

Producers decide whether or not to apply for the label once the EU publishes criteria for the product group in the Official Journal. The scheme is not mandatory but, rather, depends on market pressure to bring about change. The voluntary nature ensures that it does not create a barrier to trade. Foreign and Community producers may sell products within the EU markets without the EU eco-label.

WHAT PRODUCTS ARE CURRENTLY COVERED BY THE ECO-LABEL SCHEME?

The scheme covers the following range of products:

- copying paper
- dishwashers
- dishwashing detergents
- footwear
- laundry detergents
- light bulbs
- mattresses
- paints and varnishes
- personal computers
- portable computers
- refrigerators
- soil-improvers
- textile products
- tissue papers
- washing machines.

APPLYING FOR THE LABEL

Each member state of the EU has a designated Competent Body responsible for receiving applications from manufacturers or importers for the award of the eco-label to their products. The Competent Body decides on standard application forms with explanatory notes based on the product group definitions and ecological criteria that have been previously adopted. Each decision to award an eco-label to an individual product must first be cleared with the Competent Bodies in all member states (during a 30-day period). This clearance ensures the ability of a successful applicant to enjoy Community-wide recognition of the eco-label award.

A successful applicant signs a contract with the Competent Body for the use of the eco-label for the remaining period of validity of the ecological criteria. Once successful, applicants may use the official flower logo on their approved product. The UK Competent Body is based in DEFRA.

Fees

There are two elements to the fees companies pay for the eco-label:

1. An application fee of between €300 and €1,300 with a possible 25 per cent reduction for SMEs.

2. An annual fee of 0.15 per cent of annual volume of sales at ex-factory prices, at a minimum of €500 and a maximum of €25,000. SMEs can benefit from a 25 per cent reduction. There is a further 15 per cent reduction for EMAS/ISO-certified companies, and possible reductions for first movers with a cumulative reduction limit of 50 per cent.

Remember that you have to pay any testing or verification fees in addition to the application and annual fees.

FIVE STEPS TO SUCCESSFUL ECO-LABELLING

1. Submitting your application

- Select the category for which the application is sought from those covered by the scheme.
- Contact the National Competent Body where the product is produced or first imported. It will analyse your needs, provide you with technical support and analyse financial conditions.
- To apply, provide all the necessary information and test results to prove that your product complies with the ecological and performance criteria.

2. Evaluation of your application

The National Competent Body will assess your application against the relevant ecological and performance criteria and your manufacturing facility may be inspected for compliance with the criteria.

3. Receiving the eco-label

The Competent Body will authorise you to use the eco-label on your product and product advertising – if your product meets the relevant ecological and performance requirements. You must pay your fee in advance of the label's use.

4. Compliance monitoring

Competent Bodies may inspect factories and carry out product tests to guarantee the integrity of the eco-label.

5. Promoting your efforts

You should promote your product actively through advertising, promotional materials and other marketing initiatives including point of sales promotions. You should check with the Competent Body to find out if there are any supporting measures in place at the time of your successful application.

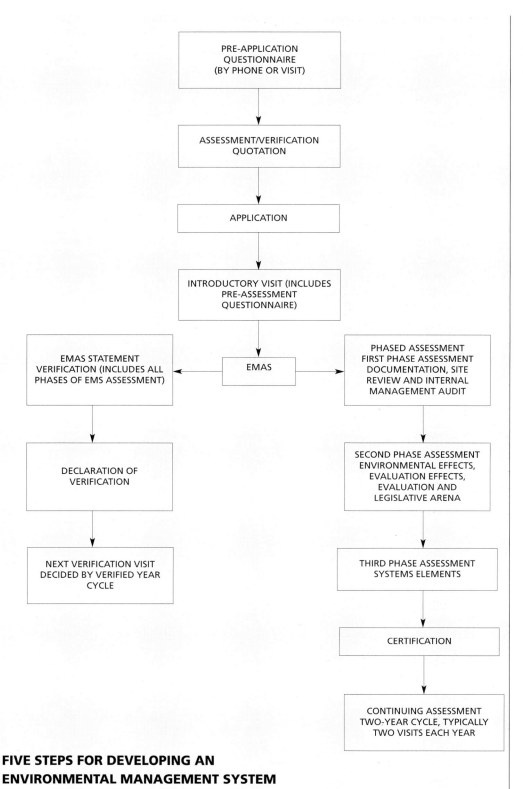

FIVE STEPS FOR DEVELOPING AN
ENVIRONMENTAL MANAGEMENT SYSTEM

WHAT SHOULD YOU DO NEXT?

Every business should take a regular look at improving its performance. External standards and registration schemes give you a target to aim for and help to put a structure on how you achieve it. SMEs should seriously consider going after one, if not all three, of the standards above.

Some steps you should take include:

- Find out if any of your major customers are interested in working with you through Project Acorn.
- If you are a manufacturer, see if your products are covered by the eco-label scheme. Get the product documentation and start working towards meeting the requirements.
- Contact your local business associations, business/environment clubs and see what support you might get for going after EMAS or ISO 14000 standards.
- No matter what – start preparing your EMS.

CONTACT INFORMATION

EMAS

The EMAS Competent Body,
Institute of Environmental Management and Assessment,
St. Nicholas House,
70 Newport,
Lincoln LN1 3DP
Telephone: + (44) (0)1522 540 069
Facsimile: + (44) (0)1522 540 090

You can get details of IEMA and link to the EMAS Competent Body information on the Web by connecting to: http://www.iema.net

There is more information on EMAS on the EU's site at:
http//europa.eu/comm/environment/emas/.
You will find a list of UK verifiers on this website, too.

ISO

BSI Group Headquarters,
389 Chiswick High Road,
London W4 4AL
Telephone: +(44) (0)20 8996 9000
Facsimile: +(44) (0) 20 8996 7400
e-mail: info@bsi-global.com
Website: www.bsi-global.com

You will find the address of their office nearest to you on their website.

Acorn

For more information about the Acorn Project, contact the Co-ordinator on:
Telephone: +44 (0) 20 8996 7665
e-mail: Project_Acorn@bsi-global.com

Eco-Label

The UK Competent Body is:
DEFRA,
Zone 6/E10,
Ashdown House,
123 Victoria Street,
London SW1E 6DE
Telephone: +44 (0) 207 944 6576
Facsimile: +44 (0) 207 944 6559

NOTES TO CHAPTER 9

i   BSI website, http://www.bsi-global.com British Standards Institute's website, http://www.bsi-global.com

ii   European Union's website, http://europa.eu.int/index_en.htm

iii   European Union's website, http://europa.eu.int/index_en.htm

iv   European Union's website, http://europa.eu.int/index_en.htm

v   British Standards Institute environmental brochure, available on-line at http://www.bsi-global.com (courtesy of BSI)

vi   Eco-label website, http://europa.eu.int/comm/environment/ecolabel

Appendix

YOUR TOP TEN INFORMATION SOURCES

In this section, we list the key ten information sources that you'll need to help you start improving your environmental practice. These organisations have websites and they, in turn, have links to other sites of interest.

Business in the Environment (BiE)

BiE, established in 1989, is a business-led campaign for environmental responsibility. Its aim is to get companies to recognise that environmental responsibility is an essential part of business excellence. BiE produces an annual index that benchmarks the corporate engagement of the top UK listed companies. SMEs are likely to be interested in their range of research reports and best practice guides, DIY workbooks, directories and training packs. BiE has active teams in Northern Ireland, the West Midlands and Yorkshire, and The Humber.

Business in the Environment,
137 Shepherdess Walk,
London N1 7RQ
Telephone: + 44 (0) 870 600 2482
Facsimile: + 44 (0) 207 7253
e-mail: bie@bitc.org.uk
Website: www.business-in-environment.org.uk

Department of the Environment, Food and Rural Affairs (DEFRA)

We describe DEFRA's functions in Chapter 4. Its contact details are:
Nobel House,
17 Smith Square,
London SW1P 3JR
Telephone: +44(0) 207 7238 5609
Facsimile: +44(0) 207238 5529
Website: www.defra.gov.uk

Environment Agency

You'll find a full description of the Agency in Chapter 4. Its contact details are:
Environment Agency,
Rio House,
Waterside Drive, Aztec West,
Almondsbury,
Bristol BS12 4UD
Telephone: +44 (0) 845 933 3111
Facsimile: +44 (0) 1454 624409
Website: http//www.environment-agency.gov.uk
Emergency Hotline: 0800807060
Floodline: +44(0) 845 988 1188

Environmental Data Services Ltd (ENDS)

ENDS is an independent publisher producing a range of information and analysis. Its products include:

- The *ENDS Report* – a monthly journal published electronically and in print covering environmental news and analysis
- *ENDS Environmental Daily*, a European environmental, electronic, news service delivered daily and also posted on the Web
- *ENDS Environmental Consultancy Directory*, a directory of UK consultancies published electronically and in print and updated monthly.

Environmental Data Services Ltd,
40 Bowling Green Lane,
London EC1R 0NE
Tel: +44 (0) 20 7814 5300
Fax: +44 (0) 20 7415 0106
e-mail: post@ends.co.uk
Website: www.ends.co.uk

Envirowise

Envirowise is a Government-funded programme offering free, independent advice on practical ways to minimise waste. It provides:

- the environment and energy helpline – one hour of free advice
- publications – case studies, best practice guides and reference notes on waste minimisation
- fast-track visits – which are free, on-site waste reviews with Envirowise consultants who will help you to identify and realise savings quickly
- waste minimisation clubs a chance for local and regional companies to meet and share best practice in waste minimisation
- events – best practice seminars and practical workshops.

The Environment and Energy Helpline: 0800 585794
Website: www.envirowise.gov.uk

Groundwork ebs

Groundwork Environmental Business Services (ebs) provides practical support, advice, information and training to companies on environmental business issues. It aims to encourage companies and their employees to be more aware or their environmental impact on the community. Groundwork is a national organisation of over 40 local Trusts.

As a member of a Groundwork business club, association or network, you'll gain access to many of the tools needed to help your business achieve cost savings and environment improvements.

Groundwork ebs,
85-87 Cornwall Street,
Birmingham B3 3BY
Telephone: +44 (0) 121 2368565
Facsimile: +44 (0) 121 236 7356
e-mail: ebs@groundwork.org.uk
Website: www.groundwork.org.uk

Institute of Environmental Management and Assessment (IEMA)

The IEMA is an independent membership body that provides recognition and support to environmental professionals, combining the disciplines of environmental management, auditing and assessment, encompassing both public and private sectors.

With approximately 6,000 members, the IEMA is the leading UK membership organisation dedicated to the promotion of the goal of sustainable development and to the professional development of individuals involved in environmental management and assessment. It offers membership at three levels: Affiliate, Associate and Full. Its services include:

- meetings
- publications including the environmentalist magazine
- training and development.

Institute of Environmental Management and Assessment
St Nicholas House,
70 Newport,
Lincoln LN1 3DP
Telephone: +44 (0) 1522540 069
Facsimile: +44 (0) 1522 540 090
Website: http//www.iema.net

Northern Ireland Environment and Heritage Service (NIEHS)

You'll find details of NIEHS and its work earlier, in Chapter 4. Its contact details are:

Environment and Heritage Service,

Directorate and Corporate Affairs,

Commonwealth House,

35 Castle Street,

Belfast BT1 1GU

Telephone: +44(0) 28 9025 1477

Facsimile: +44(0) 28 9054 6660

e-mail: ca@doeni.gov.uk

Website: www.ehsni.gov.uk

Scottish Environment Protection Agency SEPA

Details of SEPA are included in the main text.

Its contact details are:

Head Office,

Erskine Court,

Castle Business Park,

Stirling FK9 4TR

Telephone: +44(0) 1786 457700

Emergency hotline: 0800 807060

Facsimile: +44(0) 1786 446885

e-mail: info@sepa.org.uk

Website: www.sepa.org.uk

Stationery Office

(Mail, telephone and fax orders only)
PO Box 29, Norwich NR3 1GN
General enquiries 0870 600 5522
Fax orders 0870 600 5533
Email orders book.orders@theso.co.uk
Internet http://www.clicktso.com

The Stationery Office Bookshops
123 Kingsway, London WC2B 6PQ
020 7242 6393 Fax 020 7242 6394
68-69 Bull Street, Birmingham B4 6AD
0121 236 9696 Fax 0121 236 9699
33 Wine Street, Bristol BS1 2BQ
0117 9264306 Fax 0117 9294515
9-21 Princess Street, Manchester M60 8AS
0161 834 7201 Fax 0161 833 0634
16 Arthur Street, Belfast BT1 4GD
028 9023 8451 Fax 028 9023 5401
The Stationery Office Oriel Bookshop
18-19 High Street, Cardiff CF1 2BZ
029 2039 5548 Fax 029 2038 4347
71 Lothian Road, Edinburgh EH3 9AZ
0870 606 5566 Fax 0870 606 5588

Accredited Agents
(See Yellow Pages)

and through good booksellers

ABBREVIATIONS

ACBE Advisory Committee on Business and the Environment

BAT Best available technology

BATNEEC Best available technology not entailing excessive cost

BiE Business in the Environment

BSI British Standards Institute

CAC Command and control measures

CBI Confederation of British Industry

CDM Clean Development Mechanism

CITES Convention on International Trade in Endangered Species of Wild Fauna and Flora

COPA Control of Pollution Act

DEFRA Department for the Environment, Food & Rural Affairs

DTI Department for Trade and Industry

EAP Environmental Action Programme

EEA European Environment Agency

EIONET European Environmental Information and Observation Network

EMAS Environmental Management and Audit System

EMS Environmental Management System

ENDS Environmental Data Services Limited

EPI Environmental Protection Indicators

EPO Environment Protection Officer

EU European Union, and used to refer to the Common Market, the European Economic Community and the European Community

EUEB European Union Eco-labelling Board

FM Flexibility Mechanisms

GATT General Agreement on Tariffs and Trade

IEMA Institute of Environmental Management and Assessment

IPC Integrated Pollution Control

IPPC Integrated Pollution Prevention and Control

ISO International Organisation for Standards

LAAPC Local Authority Air Pollution Control

LAPC Local Air Pollution Control

MBI Market-based Instruments

NAZ Noise Abatement Zone

NDPB Non-Departmental Public Body

NERC Natural Environment Research Council

NIEHS Northern Ireland Environment and Heritage Service

OECD Organisation for Economic Co-operation and Development

PPC Pollution Prevention and Control

PPP The polluter pays principle

RCEP Royal Commission on Environmental Pollution

SBRI Small Business Reseach Initiative

SEPA Scottish Environmental Protection Agency

SME Small- and medium- (sized) enterprises

UNCSD United Nations Commission for Sustainable Development

UNEP United Nations Environment Programme

WEEE Waste Electrical and Electronic Equipment

WEFU Welsh European Funding Office

WTO World Trade Organisation

Index